An American Family Since 1630

Vol. I – Paternal Ancestors

Shomberg-Domaszek-Disher-Ostrowski

Ronilda P. S. Shomberg

Also by the Author

The Pinel Family – From France to Brazil
ISBN 10: 1492766844
ISBN-13: 978-1492766841
Published September 2013, EUA

A Família Pinel – Da França ao Brasil
Edição em Português
ISBN 10: 1492862851
ISBN-13: 978-1492862857
Published October 2013

To protect their privacy, no detailed information will be entered for individuals born in 1950's and later.

Cover photo: The Wisconsin River by John Shomberg

ISBN 13: 978-1495201158
ISBN-10: 1495201155

DEDICATION

I dedicate this book to my husband John Shomberg, his mother Yvonne
Bentle Shomberg and the Dishers, Bentles, Pomeroys, Trumbulls,
Chandlers, Keeps, Cotanchs, Coltons, Griswold, Wolcotts, Williamsons,
Wyckoffs, Van Pelts and many others who made this family and this
country.

CONTENTS

PREFACE

"This shall be written for the generations that come after"

This is the story of my husband John Shomberg's family. My mother-in-law Yvonne Marie Shomberg (Bentle) researched her side of the family for years, she spent many hours copying records, by hand, from the libraries, archives and genealogical societies around Wisconsin. Her boxes of handwritten notes, newspapers clippings, photos and more are gone now but her work did not vanish. She collaborated with others doing the same research and her efforts were acknowledged in various genealogical publications.

My research is stored in my computer but I don't want it to be gone when I am. I wanted to collect mine and Yvonne's notes all in a book to be available for the next generations.

The family has a long lineage starting with the first settlers, surviving Native American attacks and serving this country in the Revolutionary War, Civil War, World War I, World War II, Korean War and Vietnam War.

The list of family names is long and each has a story to tell. I hope to do them justice.

Ronilda Pinel de Sousa Shomberg

Florida, 2014

John Gordon Shomberg

Father
John Victor Shomberg

Mother
Yvonne Marie Bentle

Father's father
Bernard Casimir Shomberg

Father's mother
Anna Disher

Mother's father
Walter Albert Bentle

Mother's mother
Clara Myrtle Gordon

Father's paternal grand-father	Father's paternal grand-mother	Father's maternal grand-father	Father's maternal grand-mother	Mother's paternal grand-Father	Mother's paternal grand-mother	Mother's maternal grand-father	Mother's maternal grand-mother
Joseph Frank Shomberg	Frances Bronystawa Domaszck	Lawrence Florian Disher	Mathilda Ostrowski	William F. Bentle	Louise Eliza Julius	John W. Gordon	Bertha Mae Keep

1. INTRODUCTION

The Shombergs are a very large family with deep roots reaching back to the first settlers in 1630 (thru the maternal line to be feature in the next Volume). This is the story of this family through history. It contains all that we know about the numerous family lines that came together in my husband and his brothers and sisters.

Going back to the 1600's and forward, I counted 79 individuals that created the families in this book. Today the tree counts 950 people in the direct line to my husband. Most cousins are not included, the older generations due to lack of information and the newer generations due to privacy issues.

But all those lines are not so different. In instances where families lived for generations in the same general location, and where other families were scarce, intermarriage was so common (as in the case of the Chandlers and Abbotts in the 1600's) that a single family might be intertwined with certain other families, and itself, many times over. It was common for brothers of one family marry sisters of another family, therefore creating double grandparents, double cousins, etc.

Due to the number of individuals involved and with the intermarriages, confusion is inevitable, with that, it will be helpful to have a print out of family tree handy. I will try to make it easier by displaying the four branches of the most current ancestors in two or more volumes and in each volume further dividing it into chapters when necessary.

The four main families are the Shombergs, the Dishers, the Bentles and the Gordons, which are my husband John's grandparents.

2. POLISH OR GERMANS

Who declared to the immigration authorities that they were born in Poland?

The emigration occurred after the partitions, when Poland did not exist on the map of Europe. Poles who were born in Poland were registered as being born in Germany, Russia or Austria. Only those who positively insisted that they were Poles were reported as such. Also counted were those who did not use regional names such as Galicia, Prussia, Pomerania, but clearly insisted that they were Polish. In other words, only people who were clearly conscious of their Polish origin were included in those statistics.

The situation was not clear. After all, the fact was that Poland did not exist, and it was difficult for American immigration officials to specify that some German, Russian or Austrian citizens should be listed as Poles.

Things only got worse when the immigrants settle down and started to respond to the Census takers. It is important to keep in mind that the census taker did not always get his or her information from the family itself but from (possibly uninformed) neighbors or others; that persons living together were not necessarily related; and that many errors were made in recording. Throughout this research the country of origins of the same individuals has been recorded as Prussia, Germany or Poland in different Census years. Their names have been misspelled and in one case even the race was change (The 1905 Wisconsin Census describe Joseph Shomberg and his entire family as "Mulatto").

The Census takers were also required to list the family members (and their residences and their ages) as of the official date of the census, not the day it was taken. Persons living on that date but since deceased were to be listed; persons born after that day were to be omitted.

At the time of the Shombergs, Dombrowski, Dishers emigration (1820-1880), their land was part of the Prussian Empire. The Polish–Lithuanian Empire ended about 1772 with the take over from Prussia. Not until 1919 did it become part of Germany or Poland. Below is the list of their "technically" derived countries of origins, how they really defined themselves we will never know for sure but the descendants eventually settled in one or the other.

Dates and places of major events in the Shomberg-Domaszek life

1820	Dombrowski, Augustin	Rzeszow, Podkarpackie[1]

1826	Disher, Franz	Podjazy, Kartuzy, Gdansk[2]
1828	Wosnick, Marianna	Podjazy, Kartuzy, Gdansk[2]
1830	Shomberg, Martin	Zelistrzewo, Tw Pormoskie[3]
1844	Dombrowski, Emilia	Borek, Karthaus, Gdansk[4]
1846	Disher, Jacob	Podjazy, Kartuzy, Gdansk[2]
1857	Shomberg-Kaczor marriage	Puck, Pormorskie[5]
1867	Shomberg, Joseph	Wejherowo[6]
1870	Disher-Dombrowski marriage	Suleczyno, Kartuzy, Gdansk[7]
1878	Disher, Lawrence	Cieszenie, Kartuzy, Gdansk[9]

1 - Rzeszow, Podkarpackie, in 1772, following first partition of Poland, Rzeszów became part of the Austrian Empire, to which it belonged for 146 years. It was occupied by the Russians from the fall of 1914 till May 1915. In November 2nd 1918 pledged its allegiance to the Polish state. **According to this, Augustin Dombrowski was born Austrian and emigrated as a Austrian.**

2 - Village of Podjazy, Kartuzy, Gdansk is part of an area administered by Pomerania. From 1806 was under the ruling of Prussia. It became part of the German Empire in 1871. In 1919 was divided between Poland and Germany. Many of the German Pomeranians immigrated to the United States in 1820, especially to the state of Wisconsin. **Franz Disher, Marianna Wosnick and Jacob Disher were born Prussians. Jacob emigrated when under German ruling.**

3 - Żelistrzewo is a village in the administrative district of Gmina Puck, within Puck County, Pomeranian Voivodeship, in northern Poland. _ 1815 to Prussia. 1871 to German Empire. 1919 to Poland. **Martin Shomberg was also born Prussian.**

5 - Puck, Pormorskie. See above[3], **Martin and Marianna were married under German ruling**

6 - Neustadt/Wejherowo – 1818 to Western Prussia. 1867 to German Federation. 1878 to Western Prussia. 1920 to Poland. **Joseph Frank Shomberg was born German but he was under Prussian ruling when emigrated.**

4, 7, 9 - Village of Borek, Suleczyno, Cieszenie in Kartuzy (Karthaus), Gdansk. Was part of Pomerania/Poland up to 1772 when was incorporated to West Prussia/Germany, and 1920 back to Poland. **Lawrence and his mother Emilia were born during Prussia/Germany rule and emigrated as such.**

Poland 1500's before partitions.

Note the locations of the of Puck, Żelistrzewo, Wejherowo, Borel, Podjazy, Suleczyno and Rzeszow, land of the Shombergs ancestors.

Map of 1815 after the Duchy of Warsaw Partition in 1809 (dashed line) and Congress Poland in 1815 (solid line). Large shaded area: Territory of the Austrian partition annexed by the Duchy of Warsaw in 1809.

Poland no longer exists! The villages the Puck, Żelistrzewo, Wejherowo, Borel, Podjazy and Suleczyno, are now in Prussia and Rzeszow in Austria.

Stevens Point in the 1900's

Photo of Market Square where Polish farmers and their wives brought their produce and animals to market. The Square and the Main Street are on the National Register of Historic Places. Courtesy of www.pchswi.org.

3. PATERNAL ANCESTRY

Martin Shomberg[441] (1830-b1923)

Joseph Frank Shomberg[500] (1867-1943)

Marianna Kaczor[442] (1828-c1886)

Bernard Casimir Shomberg[618] (1896-1970)

John (Jan) Domaszek Sr.[378] (c1815-c1870)

Thaddeus Domaszek[443] (1836-1910)

Catherine Szult[379] (c1815-c1868)

Frances Bronystawa Domaszek[501] (1876-1936)

Marianna (Mariienna) Cyra (Cera Cyran)[444] (1843-1889)

John Victor Shomberg[737] (1926-1997)

Franz Disher[380] (1826-)

Jacob Philipp Disher[447] (1845-1931)

Marianna Anna Wosnik[381] (1828-)

Lawrence (Florian) Disher[503] (1878-1934)

Jan Dombrowski[329]

Romuald Augustin Dombrowski[382] (1824-1901)

Carl Bojan Pucdrowski[285] (1768-1828)

Julianna Bojan Pucdrowski[330]

Constantia Krecka[286]

Emilia (Emilija) Dombrowski[448] (1844-1918)

Michal Klopotek (Dabrowski)[331]

Antonina von Klopotek[383] (1819-1901)

Katarzyna "Last name unknown"[332]

Anna Disher[619] (1903-1973)

Nick Ostrowski[384]

Louis (Leon) Ostrowski[449] (1846-)

Caroline Rakowski[385]

Mathilda Ostrowski[504] (1882-1993)

Martin Kiedrowski[333] (-1857)

Andrew Kiedrowski[386] (1821-1895)

Victoria Maschke[334]

Frances Kiedrowski[450] (1860-1952)

Josephine Cybulska[387] (1834-1867)

8

4. THE SHOMBERGS

Dad's side of the family lived in Madison. Grandma and Grandpa Shomberg as well as his three brothers lived there also. Everyone on the Shomberg side were in the building business as carpenter's and contractors. Both Grandma and Grandpa Shomberg were retired, and would come by our house on occasion for the holidays. Grandpa Shomberg always had some goodies with him for the kids.

Dad eventually built a house on the west side of Madison on Tolman Terrace late 1950's. It was a pretty big split level. We always saw the grandparents at holidays, and dad always made it a point to go up to Oshkosh at least once a month.

Since Grandma and Grandpa Shomberg lived in Madison, we would often go to their house to see them. They lived just down from the capitol, and I can remember looking up the street in awe of how big the capitol was.

We moved to Airport Road, Middleton, Wisconsin, around the early 60's. It was 10 miles further west of Madison. At the time, Dad was in business with his brothers and were known as "Shomberg Builders". Again, we always saw the grandparents most months. I recall spending a couple holidays with Grandma and Grandpa Shomberg, but most of the time it was the Bentle side.

Grandpa Shomberg passed away in 1970. Grandma Shomberg lived with her son Tony in Madison, until she met another gentlemen who she married and went to Missouri in the mid 1970's. When she passed away, I remember Dad and his brother Tony going to make funeral arrangements.

By John Shomberg.

MARTIN SHOMBERG was born in 1830 in Zelistrzewo, Poland. He married **MARIANNA KACZOR** on September 27, 1857, in Puck, Poland. Marianna was born in 1828 in Poland and died about 1886.

Martin died before 1923, as shown in his son's passport application of 1923. Martin and Marianna had four children (that we know of) during their marriage:

1. Franz Adam Shomberg (10/4/1858-?)
2. Anna Maria Shomberg (4/26/1861-?)
3. Rozalia Augusta Shomberg (11/25/1863-?)
4. JOSEPH FRANK SHOMBERG (2/4/1867-9/26/1943)

Life in the US _ not sure if Martin ever came to America but there was a Martin Schomberg in the passenger list of 1881 and his son (in his passport application) also lists his arrival as 1881 at the age of 14, could he have come alone? Did he come to join others? In the June 1880 US Census, there were 24 individuals with the Schomberg last name living in Wisconsin alone.

JOSEPH FRANK SHOMBERG

When **JOSEPH FRANK SHOMBERG** was born on February 4, 1867, in Neustadt, Poland, his father, MARTIN, was 37 and his mother, MARIANNA, was 39. He married **FRANCES BRONYSTAWA DOMASZEK** and they had 14 children together between 1896 and 1917.

see Frances Domaszek and her ancestors in Chapter #5

1. Helen M Shomberg was born on 29 Aug 1896 in Wisconsin, USA. She died on 13 Nov 1955 in St. Michael's Hospital, Stevens Point, Portage County, WI USA. She married Frank Zurawski on 28 May 1917. He was born on 27 Jan 1891 in Wisconsin, USA and died on 22 Mar 1970 in St Michael's Hospital, Steven Points WI US.
   They had 4 children:
      Arthur A/Betty L Terry – 1921-1979
      Ruth E/F. Denke – 1923-1993
      Carl – 1927-? No record of family
      Rosella M – 1929-? No record of family

Notes for the Shomberg/Zurawski Family

1916 – Helen Shomberg in the Gazette

THE GAZETTE, STEVENS POINT, WISCONSIN   4/19/1916

BIG JUDGMENT

·e of Land Contract Involv-
l7,755.30 Authorized by
Judge Park.

ιdley Polytechnic Institute
′. Hammond of Peoria, Ill.,
rded a judgment of fore-
a land contract by Judge
k in circuit court here last
udgment was in the sum of
which the plaintiffs alleged
n from the defendants, Law-
.wig and wife.
ιst, 1911, the plaintiffs al-
ntract was executed provid-
e sale of 280 acres in the
ounty drainage district, in
ta, to Mr. and Mrs. Hart-
purchase price was to be
yable as follows: By erect-
ιgs on the land and paying
difference between the cost

KOUNTY SCHOOL KOLUMN

Things Here and There Pertaining
to Rural Educational Work.

(The Gazette will make this department as reg-
ular as contributions of news warrant. Teachers
and others interested are invited to send in
articles of interest for publication here, but we
must insist that communications be signed, altho
the names will no tbe published if so requested.)

SCHOOL NOTES.

Miss Ethel Marcy's school in Dist.
Jt. 9, Grant, closed on April 14 for
this year.
★Miss Helen Shomberg's school in
Dist. 6, Plover, will close Friday, Apr.
21 for the year. In the afternoon a
mothers' meeting will be held, at
which light refreshments will be
served.

to realize the up-to-date
wear. It is a collection ·
season's most desirable ς
tion from numps and slir

2.   <u>BERNARD CASIMIR SHOMBERG</u> (9/3/1896-3/3/1970)

3.   Theresa Shomberg was born on 06 Jun 1900 in Wisconsin, USA. She died on 14 Feb 1977 in Duluth, St Louis, Minnesota, USA. She married Peter Kwapick on 03 Aug 1927.

There are no record of children.

4.   Vante Shomberg was born in 1901 in Wisconsin, United States. She died before 1970.

No records of marriage or children

5.   Wanda Shomberg was born on 24 Dec 1902 in Wisconsin, USA. She died on 18 Mar 1976 in Beulah, Mercer, ND. She married Richard Arthur Walker. He was born on 10 Jan 1890 in Detroit, Becker Co., MN and died on 27 Jan 1984 in Modoc Co., California.

One child: Wanda Rose – b. 1926 in North Dakota

6.   Casmira (Myra) Shomberg was born on 01 May 1904 in Hancock, Waushara County, WI USA. She died on 01 Jul 1993 in Stevens Point, Portage, Wisconsin, United States of America. She married George A. Hansen on 20 Jun 1924. He was born on 01 Apr 1901 in Nekoosa, Wood, Wisconsin, USA and he died on 15 Oct 1980 in St Michael's Hospital, Stevens Point, Portage, WI.

They had 6 children:
Ruth B./Witkowski – 1925-2009
Elmer – 1927-1954

James H – 1929-2002, St Mary's Cemetery, Veteran Army Korean War
William – 1928-before 2009. No record of family.
Maxine L/Hetzer – 1932-2005.
Gerald/Sylvia – 1936-2005

7.	Roselyn Shomberg was born on 8/18/1905 and died Sept 1945. She married Roger H. Stitt.
	They had one child:
		Roger H Stitt Jr. – 1939-? In Illinois

8.	Cassamana Shomberg was born in Wisconsin after June 1st, 1905 and died before 1970.
	No records of marriage or children

9.	Rosa Shomberg was born about 1906 in Wisconsin and died before 1970.
	No records of marriage or children.

10.	Esther Alice Shomberg was born on 02 Jun 1907 in Wisconsin, USA. She died on 29 Jun 1930. She married Emil C. Grabowski in 1925. He was born on 09 Jan 1907 and died on 23 Aug 1991 in Foley, Baldwin, Alabama, USA.

11.	Mary A. Shomberg was born on 03 May 1909 in Wisconsin, USA. She died on 13 Nov 1956 in St. Michael's Hospital, Stevens Point, Portage Co. She married Rhode Ray Sorenson on 15 Dec 1928 in Milwaukee, Milwaukee County, WI USA. He was born on 27 Sep 1906. He died on 17 Jun 1953.
	They had 7 children:
		Rhode F – 1930-?
		Fay C/Jakusz – 1931-2010
		Ione/Hetzer – 1932-?
		Eugene – 1934-?
		Benita T/Flora – 1935-?
		Rosemary – 1938-?
		Annette – 1939-?

12.	Phylomenia (Faye) A. Shomberg was born on 27 Nov 1911 in Buena Vista, Portage County, WI USA. She died on 17 Dec 2003 in Stevens Point, Portage, Wisconsin, United States. She married George E Ressler on 16 May 1929 in St. Stephen Catholic Church, Stevens Point, Portage County, WI USA. He was born on 04 Oct 1902 and died on 15 Apr 1955.

They had 4 children:
  Patricia A/Reimann– 1932-?
  Richard/Evelyn – 1933-?
  Barbara/Berndt – 1938-?
  John D/Penny– 1940-?

Portage Obituary – December 26, 2003

Philomena "Faye" A. Ressler, 92, of 3617 Minnesota Ave., died unexpectedly Wednesday, Dec. 17, 2003, at home.

Funeral services will be held 11 a.m. Monday at Boston Funeral Home. The Rev. John Potaczek will officiate. Friends may call from 5 until 8 p.m. with a 7 p.m. rosary Sunday at the funeral home. Friends may also call after 10 a.m. Monday at the funeral home. Burial will take place at Forest Cemetery. A memorial will be established in her name later.

Faye was born Nov. 27, 1911, on the family farm in the town of Buena Vista. She was a daughter of the late Joseph and Frances Shomberg. In 1920, the family moved to Stevens Point where she attended local schools and Emerson High School.

She was married to George E. Ressler on May 16, 1929. Their first home was in the Vertiel subdivision which is now the village of Park Ridge. She served on their first election board. In 1942, she and her husband moved to McDill Township (now the village of Whiting) where she recently resided.

Her husband died in 1955. Following his death, she held several part-time jobs and then worked for Sentry Insurance until she retired in 1978.

Faye enjoyed gardening, sewing clothes for her family, making patchwork quilts, knitting and embroidery. She also enjoyed braiding and hooking rag rugs. She liked to read, was an avid Packers fan and watched all their games on TV. She liked to travel and had a wonderful companion in her younger son, John they traveled coast to coast and to Alaska.

Survivors include two sons, Richard (Evelyn) of St. Louis and John (Penny) of Leavenworth, Wash. two daughters, Patricia (Ernest) Reimann of St. Paul, Minn., and Barbara Berndt of Stevens Point seven grandchildren seven great-grandchildren and many nieces and nephews.

Besides her husband, she was preceded in death by seven sisters, Helen, Theresa, Wanda, Myra, Rose, Esther and Mary and two brothers, Bernard and Sylvester

13.   Sylvester John Shomberg was born on 24 Mar 1917 in Wisconsin, USA. He died on 15 Dec 1992 in Pewaukee, Waukesha, Wisconsin, United States. He married (1) Mary Anne Anna Wroblewski on 26 Apr 1937 in Stevens Point, Portage County, WI USA. She was born on 26 Feb 1918 in Stevens Point, Portage, Wisconsin, United States and died on 20 Feb 2006 in St Michael's Hospital, Steven Points WI US. He married (2) Elaine M Schrader on 19 Jul 1956 in Jackson, Kansas City, Missouri. She was born on 04 Sep 1915. She died on 13 Mar 1984 in Pewaukee, Waukesha, Wisconsin,

United States of America.

He had 8 children with Mary Wroblewski.:

Bernice M
Carol M
Christian
Frances M
James S
Judith A
Shirley A
Stephen – 1944-?

Joseph Shomberg later married Annastasia Bronystawa Selonka and they had two children together between 1924 and 1932.

Agnes (Anges) Shomberg was born on 23 Jul 1924. She died on 06 Jan 1998 in Green Bay, Brown, Wisconsin, United States of America. She married Raymond C Niec on 18 Jul 1942. He was born on 07 Nov 1919. He died on 05 Jun 1972 in Pitt, Wisconsin.

Alois B Shomberg was born on 07 Apr 1932. He married Geraldine R. She was born on 15 Jul 1933. She died on 09 Apr 2003 in FL

JOSEPH FRANK died on September 26, 1943, in Pulaski, Wisconsin, at the age of 76, and was buried in Oconto, Wisconsin.

Timeline for JOSEPH FRANK SHOMBERG:

1881 25 Oct at age 14: he arrived in NY, per passport application_ Departed from Bremen, Germany.
Passport issued: 11 Aug 1923.

1891 12 Jan at age 23: marriage to Frances Browystawa Domaszck at the Sacred Heart Polish Catholic Church, Polonia, Sharon, Portage Co

1895 Wisconsin, State Censuses, 1895 and 1905. In June 20, 1895, a Joe Shomberg lived in Buena Vista, Wisconsin. Census count 1 male and 1 female.

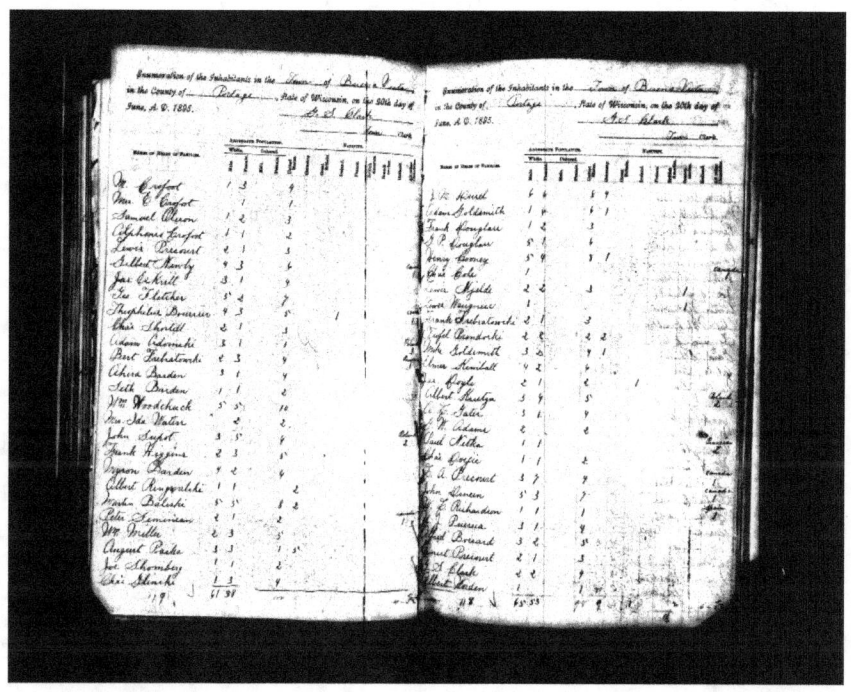

NOTE: Different arrival dates

1910 Census shows 1880,
1920 Census says 1881,
1930 Census, 1883?

1898 January 8 - Foreclosure Stevens Point Journal

First publication January 8-98-w7.

STATE OF WISCONSIN—IN CIRCUIT COURT—PORTAGE COUNTY.

Chri-tian Beck, Plaintiff against Kristoff Glin-ski, Joseph Shomberg, Frances Shomberg and William J. Leary, Defendants.

By virtue of a judgment of foreclosure and sale rendered on the 29th day of December, A. D. 1896, in the above entitled action, and duly perfected and entered of record in the office of the clerk of the circuit court for said Portage county on the 4th day of January, A. D. 1897, I shall on Wednesday, the 23d day of February. A. D. 1898, at the hour of two o'clock in the afternoon of that day, at the sheriff's office in the court house, in the city of Stevens Point, in said Portage county offer for sale and sell at public auction and vendue to the highest bidder the following describ-ed mortgaged property, or so much thereof as will be necessary to satisfy said judgment, with interest, and costs of sale. to-wit: The north-west quarter of the north-east quarter of section number twelve [12], in township number twenty-two [22] north, of range number nine [9] east, in the county of Portage and State of Wisconsin.

Dated January 6, A. D. 1898.

FRANK WHEELOCK,

18

1905 - On June 1, 1905, Joseph Shomberg was 39 years old and lived in the town of Deerfield, Wisconsin with his wife, Francis, son Bernet (sic), and 4 daughters, Hellen (sic), Thresa (sic), Vante and Casmer (sic). He is said to be a farmer born in Poland/Germany, the family live in a farmhouse which he owned, free of mortgage.

Wisconsin State Census, 1895 and 1905

1910 - On April 11 1910, Joseph F. Shomberg was 43 years old and lived in Stevens Point Rd #16, Town of Buena Vista, Portage Co., Wisconsin with his wife, Frances, son Bernard, and 6 daughters, Helen M., Theresa B., Wanda A., Wassamana, Rosa and Ester A (sic). They were married for 19 yrs. Joseph shows his year of immigration as 1880 and was a naturalized citizen. He was a farmer working of his own account. He still owned his farm free of mortgage and was able to read and write.

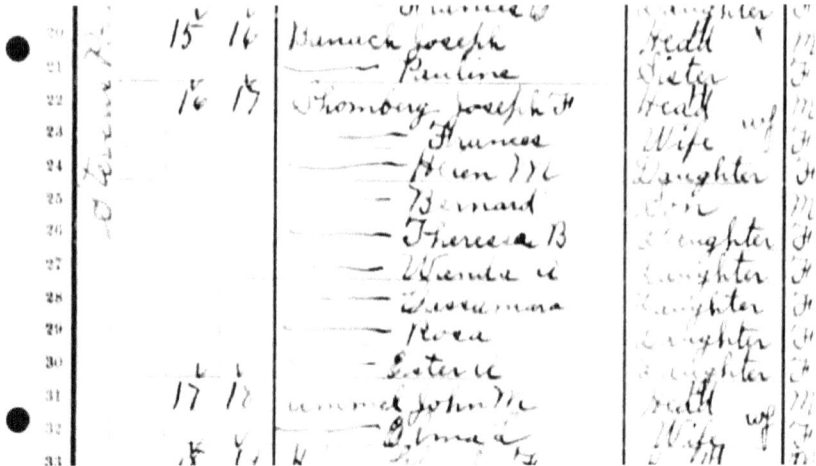

1910 United States Federal Census

1915 - Plat map of the Township of Buena Vista shows Jos Shomberg's land.

1915 Plat Map

1916, May 1 - **U.S. Naturalization Record Indexes**, 1791-1992 (Indexed in World Archives Project)

```
'S  5 1 6        -
Family name                    |   Given name or names
   Shamberg        -           |      Joseph Frank
Address                        |
   R.#1, Bancroft              |
Certificate no. (or vol. and page)  |  Title and location of court   Wis.
   p-352                       |   Cir,Portage Co,Stevens Pt
Country of birth or allegiance |      When born (or age)
   Germany                     |      1867
Date and port of arrival in U.S.    |  Date of naturalization
                               |      May 1,1916
Names and addresses of witnesses    |
```

U. S. Department of Labor Immigration and Naturalization Service   Form No. 1.1 P.

1920 United States Federal Census

On January 26, 1920, Joseph Shomberg was 52 years old and lived in Buena Vista, Portage, Wisconsin with his wife, Frances, 2 sons Bernard and Sylvester, and 6 daughters, Wanda, Kasmer (sic), Rosy (sic), Esther, Mary and Filomina (sic). His home was owned and free of mortgage. Joseph gives his year of immigration as 1881 (different from 1910 Census) and he was naturalized in 1913(also different from the naturalization records). He was able to read and write, was born in Poland and his mother tongue was Polish (he also spoke English), as was his mother and father. He was a farmer working to his own account.

16			Lila Louise	daughter		
17	Am 187 189	Shomberg Joseph	Head		1	0
18			Frances	Wife		
19	/		Bernard	son		
20	/		Wanda	daughter		
21	v		Kasmer	daughter		
22	/		Rosy	daughter		
23	v		Esther	daughter		
24	v		Mary	daughter		
25	v		Filomina	daughter		
26	v		Sylvester	son		

1921 Divorce from Frances and reconciled in 2/6/1922.
Wisconsin Rapids Daily Tribune

DIVORCE DECREE IS SET ASIDE BY JUDGE

Stevens Point—Frances Shomberg and Joseph F. Shomberg, city, who on September 24, 1921, were divorced in circuit court here, have become reconciled and today a judgment was entered setting aside the verdict. The judgment was entered at their petition.

The reconciliation did not last long...

1923, August 11 - Joseph Frank Shomberg applied for a passport to Poland where he says:

I, Joseph Frank Shomberg, a naturalized and loyal citizen of the United States, hereby apply to the Department of State, at Washington, for a passport to Poland.

I solemnly swear that I was born a Neustadt, Poland on February 4th, 1867; that my father, Martin Shomberg, was born in Poland and is now deceased; that I emigrated to the United States, sailing from Bremen, Germany about October 14th, 1881; that I resided 42 years, uninterruptedly, in the United States from 1881 to 1923 at Portage County, Wisconsin; that I was naturalized as a citizen of the United States before the Circuit Court of Portage County at Steven Point, WI on May 1st, 1916, as shown by the Certificate of Naturalization presented herewith...

...and that I am domiciled in the United States, my permanent residence being at Stevens Point, in the State of Wisconsin, where I follow the occupation of Engineer...

...I am about to go abroad temporarily...to visit relatives in Poland.

I intend to leave the United States from the port of New York on or about August 25th, 1923

(Signature of applicant.)

Joseph Frank Shomberg signature

331368

The original and each copy of an application for a passport must have attached to it a copy of the applicant's photograph. A loose signed photograph of the applicant must accompany the application.
The photographs must be on thin paper, should have a light background, and be not over three inches in size.

This blank must be completely filled out. The legal fee of one dollar, in currency or postal money order, and the applicant's certificate of naturalization must accompany the application.
The rules should be carefully read before mailing the application to the Department of State, Division of Passport Control, Washington, D. C.

[Edition of January, 1919.]

[FORM FOR NATURALIZED CITIZEN.]

DEPARTMENT OF STATE
PASS PORT
AUG 11 1923
ISSUED
WASHINGTON

UNITED STATES OF AMERICA,
STATE OF Wisconsin } ss:
COUNTY OF Portage

I, Joseph Frank Shomberg, a NATURALIZED AND LOYAL CITIZEN OF THE UNITED STATES, hereby apply to the Department of State, at Washington, for a passport.

To Poland

I solemnly swear that I was born at Neustadt, Poland
on February, 4th, 1867.; that my father,
Martin Thomberg, was
(Name.)
born in Poland, and is now residing at Deceased;
(Country.)
that I emigrated to the United States, sailing from Bremen, Germany about
October 14th, 1881; that I resided 42 years, uninterruptedly, in the United States,
from 1881 to 1923 at Portage County, Wisconsin; that I was
naturalized as a citizen of the United States before the Circuit
Court of Portage County at Stevens Point, Wis.
on May 1st, 1916, as shown by the Certificate of Naturalization presented herewith;
that I am the IDENTICAL PERSON described in said Certificate; that I have resided outside the United
States since my naturalization at the following places for the following periods:

_____, from _____ to _____,
_____, from _____ to _____,
and that I am domiciled in the United States, my permanent residence being at Stevens Point,
in the State of Wisconsin, where I follow the occupation of Engineer.
My last passport was obtained from _____
_____ and was _____ I am about
(Date.) (Disposition of passport.)
to go abroad temporarily, and intend to return to the United States within One
[months] with the purpose of residing and performing the duties of citizenship therein; and I desire
[years]
a passport for use in visiting the countries hereinafter named for the following purpose:

Poland
(Name of country.)   Visit Relatives
(Object of visit.)

_____
(Name of country.)   _____
(Object of visit.)

_____
(Name of country.)   _____
(Object of visit.)

I intend to leave the United States from the port of New York
(Port of departure.)
sailing on board the Do not know on about August 25th, 19 23
(Name of vessel.)   (Date of departure.)

OATH OF ALLEGIANCE.

Further, I do solemnly swear that I will support and defend the Constitution of the United States against all enemies, foreign and domestic; that I will bear true faith and allegiance to the same; and that I take this obligation freely, without any mental reservation or purpose of evasion: So help me God.

Joseph Frank Shomberg
(Signature of applicant.)

Sworn to before me this _____ day
of August, 19 23.

[SEAL OF COURT]

FEE $... AUG 11 1923
1983
J. E. Niban
Clerk of the Circuit Court at Stevens Point, Wis. 1937
[OVER.]

24

1924 – Joseph Schomberg (sic) arrived in New York, New York, on May 28, 1924, at the age of 56. With his new bride Anna.

New York, Passenger Lists, 1820-1957

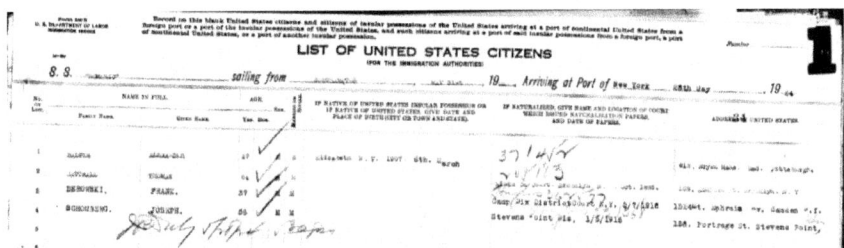

List of United States Citizens

SS "Homeric" sailing from Southampton, May 21st, 1924. Arriving at port of New York on May 28th, 1924.

Schomberg (sic) Joseph – 56 yrs old, married, male – naturalized in Stevens Point, WI, 1/5/1916 – Address: 158 Portrage (sic) St, Stevens Point, WI.

List or Manifest of Alien Passengers for the United States

Schomberg (sic) Anna – 36 yrs old, female, married, housewife, able to read and write in Polish, Nationality: Polish, from Cielbowo (sic), Reda, Poland. Address in Poland: 15 Tuasky St, Wejberowo, Poland. Final destination: Stevens Point, WI.

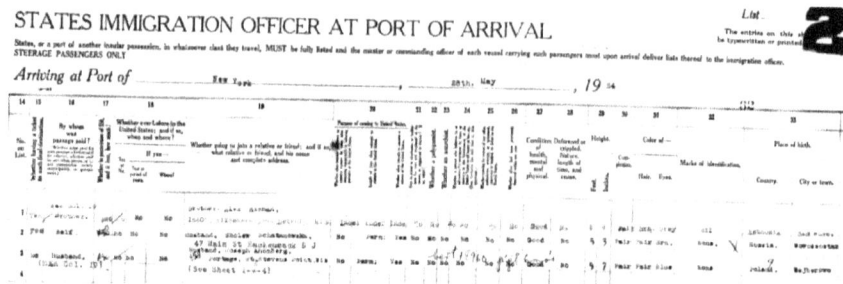

States Immigration Officer at Port of Arrival

Passage paid by husband, Joseph Ahomberg (sic) of 158 Portage St, Stevens Point, WI. She has never been to the States and has $50.00 in her possession. She intends to live here permanently and became a citizen of the US. She does not have or been treated for any illness; she is not a polygamist nor an anarchist; ... Mental and physical health: good. Height: 5'7', fair complexion, color of hair: fair, color of eyes: blue, etc.

SS Homeric

26

1927 US City Directories – Stevens Point

Shomberg Frances (wid Jos F) residing at 160 Superior Ave.
Shomberg Jos F (Anna) laborer residing at 125 Hardig Ave
Shomberg Mary – student, same address as mother Frances.

US City Directories

1930 United States Federal Census

In April 11, 1930, Joseph Shomberg was 59 yrs old and lived in 87 Gale St, Oconto City, Oconto, WI with his wife Anna and daughter Agnes. He rented this home for $9.00 a month. They were both born in Poland of Polish parents. They spoke Polish at home. Year of immigration for Joseph: 1883 (another different date), for Anna: 1924. Both are naturalized citizens and able to speak English. His occupation is listed as Fireman in a saw mill. He was actually employed and was not a veteran.

1930 United States Federal Census

1940 United States Federal Census.

On April 1st, 1940, Joseph Schomberg was 73 yrs old and lived in Pittsfield, Brown Co, WI with his wife Anna, son Alois and daughter Agnes. According to the Census, Joseph attended school up to 8th grade. Anna attended school up to 4th grade. In 1935 they resided at the same address. He worked as an operator on a farm for 40 hrs a week, 52 weeks a year and shows no income.

1940 United States Federal Census

1943 September 26 – Joseph Frank Shomberg died in Pulasky, Brown Co, WI and was buried at the Polish National Cemetery in Oconto, WI.

His tombstone has the inscription: Father Joseph Shomberg 1867-1943.

BERNARD CASIMIR SHOMBERG

When BERNARD CASIMIR SHOMBERG was born on September 3, 1896, in Wisconsin, his father, JOSEPH, was 29 and his mother, FRANCES, was 19. He married **ANNA DISHER** on January 4, 1922. They had eight children in 15 years. He died on March 3, 1970, in Madison, Wisconsin, at the age of 73, and was buried in Memory Gardens, Madison, WI.

See Anna Disher and her ancestors in Chapter #6

Bernard and Anna had eight children:
1. Raymond Shomberg (10/3/1923 – 9/23/1925)

Stevens Point Daily Journal Friday, September 25, 1925 Obituary Convulsions Cause Death Raymond, the three year old son of Mr. and Mrs. Bernard Shomberg of Buena Vista, died very suddenly on Wednesday and will be buried from St. Bronislava's church at Plover Saturday morning at 8 o'clock with interment in the parish cemetery. The child was taken with convulsions early Wednesday and passed away at 5 p.m. A primary cause of death is also given as cholera infantum.

2. Lorraine Mary (Valerie) Shomberg was born on 14 Mar 1924 in Portage, Wisconsin, United States. She died on 02 Aug 2008 in Rothschild, Marathon, Wisconsin, USA. She married Lester Buelow on 10 Feb 1951. He was born on 01 Dec 1924. He died on 06 Nov 1996.
They had 2 children:
Calvin/Jacci Woodward – 1952-?
Debra L/Kevin Rick – 1957-?

Portage Obituary – Aug 4, 2008
She was born March 14, 1924, in Portage County to the late Bernard and Mathilda (Discher) Shomberg (SHOULD BE ANNA DISHER). On Feb. 10, 1951, Lorraine married Lester Buelow in Stevens Point. They were longtime residents of Rothschild, raising their two children, Calvin and Debbie. Lorraine had been employed with the D.C. Everest School District in the food service department before retiring. Her faith in God was very important to her, regularly worshiping at Mount Calvary Lutheran Church, Rothschild. Lorraine took great comfort in the loving care she gave her family. She was a wonderful cook and loved baking goodies for them. Her hobbies included reading, canning her own vegetables from her garden, as well as listening and dancing to polka music.

Survivors include her son, Calvin (Jacci) Buelow of Mosinee; her daughter, Debbie (Kevin) Rick of Weston; four grandchildren, Christopher and Daniel Buelow, Courtney (Chad) Hoeppner, Lance Rick; one great-granddaughter, Cambrie Hoeppner; two sisters, Irene (Larry) Lange of Florida and Theresa (Bennie) DeMerchant of Brazil, South America; and three brothers, Bernie (Linda) Shomberg of Denver, Tony (Donna) Shomberg of Madison and Joe (Friend-Priscilla) Shomberg of Winter Haven, Fla. Lorraine was preceded in death by Lester on Nov. 6, 1996, and two brothers, John and Raymond Shomberg.

3.   JOHN VICTOR SHOMBERG (8/29/1926 – 5/17/1997)

4.   Irene Shomberg was born on 04 Jun 1929 in Milwaukee, Milwaukee County, WI USA. She married Lawrence (Larry) Lange. He was born in 1930 in Oconomowoc, Waukesha, Wisconsin, USA. No record of children.

5.   Bernard Vincent Shomberg was born on 19 Jul 1932 in Portage, Wisconsin, United States. He died on 21 Oct 2008 in Littleton, Douglas, Colorado, United States. He married Linda Catherine Power on 11 Jul 1981 in Vernon, Wisconsin. She was born in 1944.
They had 4 children:
> Debbie (Tom) of Nairobi, Kenya
> Jeff (Ann) of Ft Meyers, FL
> Curt (Connie) of Middleton
> Christian of Wichita, Kansas

6.   Theresa Shomberg was born about 1936 in Wisconsin. She married Bennie DeMerchant on 22 Jul 1961 in Ramsey, Minnesota. He was born on 31 Jan 1941

Note for Bennie and Theresa:

Bennie DeMerchant, left NB Canada for Saint Paul, MN in 1959 where he acquired his private pilot license, married Theresa Shomberg a Bible school teacher from Wisconsin and graduated from ABI. After a short three year pastoral stage in New Brunswick they arrived as UPCI missionaries in Manaus, capital of the huge Amazon state in northern Brazil in 1965 where they live to present. Bennie combines evangelism tools of a Cessna 172 and 206 single engine seaplanes kept in a floating hangar in a lake off the Amazon near Manaus with a fleet of wooden boats, aluminum canoes, portable cement block forms and trained workers to plant churches in the Amazon cities, towns, villages, islands, lakes and among Indian tribes. A UPC convention Center has been built in East Manaus that accommodates up to seven thousand people for special events. Theresa DeMerchant, national director of Bible schools, coordinates the work of translating, printing and curriculum for 65 Bible school locations with 204 teachers, 1,121 registered 2-year students, and 4,500 alumni. This vital training work has been liberally supported by Ladies Ministries of UPCI since 1972. Many trained youth have left these schools to open up new works in many towns. DeMerchant was elected Bishop of the UPC of Brazil in 1989 presently with 32 districts and 1,200 churches and congregations. About 750 churches are in the Amazon Basin, the northern half of Brazil, a hot equatorial zone equivalent to the area of the USA east of the Mississippi River. Most areas have no roads. The natural road is the rivers to many places reached in days by boats otherwise only reached by air. Full Throttle, (a Pentecostal Publishing House publication) records their adventures, challenges and fears in flying thousands of hours to open the world's largest rain forest area for His kingdom

7.   Anthony Myron Shomberg was born August 17, 1937 in Wisconsin. He married (1) Carolee M Haack on 21 Oct 1961 in Luther Memorial Church.

Capital Times Saturday, July 15, 1961 *Carolee M. Haack Is Fiancée of Anthony Myron Shomberg AND MRS. Herman J. Haack, M i d d l e t o n, announce the engagement and forthcoming marriage" of their daughter, Carolee Marlene, to Anthony Myron Shomberg, son of Mr. and Mrs. Bernard C. Shomberg, 139 S. Hancock St., formerly of Stevens Point. The bride-elect is art director for Silk Screen Advertising Co., and her fiancé is associated with Shomberg Builders and Designers. The wedding will be Oct. 21 in' Luther Memorial Church.*

He married (2) Donna Sharon Valenza in July 1985.

8.   Joseph M. Shomberg was born on October 12, 1939 in Wisconsin. No record of marriage or children.

Timeline for BERNARD SHOMBERG:

1905 – In June 1, 1905, Bernet (sic) Shomberg was 8 yrs old and lived in Deerfield, Wisconsin with his father, mother and 4 sisters.

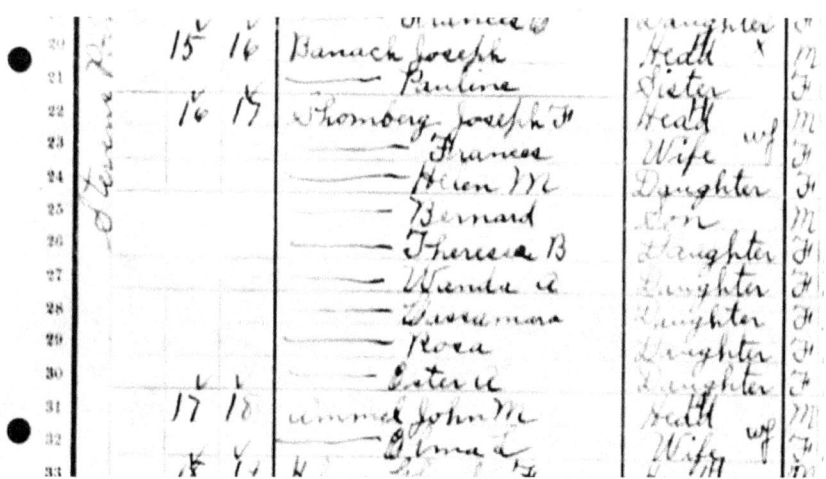

Wisconsin, State Censuses, 1895 and 1905

1910 – In April 16, 1910 Bernard was 11 yrs old and lived at Stevens Point Rd #16, Buena Vista, Portage, WI with his father, mother and 6 sisters. He had attended school since September of 1909 and was able to read and write.

1910 United States Federal Census.

33

1918 - Sept 12, 1918. Bernard Casimir Shomberg was living in Portage, Wisconsin, when he registered for the World War I draft. He was of medium build, medium height, grey eyes and brown hair.

U.S., World War I Draft Registration Cards, 1917-1918

Bernard's signature. Note middle name Casmar.

1920 - In January 26, 1920, Bernard Shomberg was 21 years old and lived in Buena Vista, Wisconsin with his father, mother, brother, and 6 sisters. He no longer attended school and worked as laborer at his home farm.

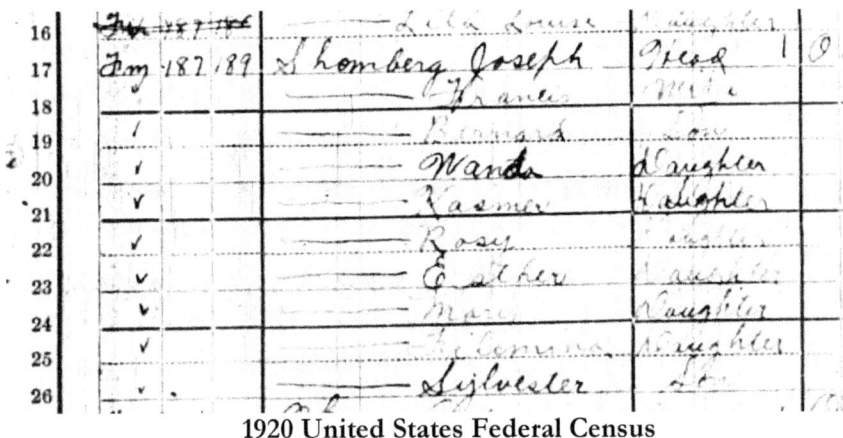

1920 United States Federal Census

1922 – In January 4th, 1922 he married ANNA DISHER at the St. Bronislava Church, Plover, Portage Co., WI.

1927- Bernard and his brother-in-law John Disher got into some mischievous behavior and made the news. Although there was a 10 year age difference, they must have been good friends, the 1930 Census shows John Disher living with Bernard as boarder.

Stevens Point Daily Journal
Monday, December 5, 1927
TROUTING BY HAND IN DRAINAGE DITCH RESULTS IN FINES

As the result of investigations by S. E. Browning, a deputy sheriff, and Harry E. Brooks, secretary of the Izaak Walton league, two men were fined in county court this morning on charges of taking trout during the closed season.

The two were Bernard Shomberg and John Disher, both residents near the drainage district, who were taken into custody on Sunday afternoon at the head waters of the Isherwood ditch in Buena Vista and brought to county jail.

Pleading guilty to charges of capturing and killing trout during the closed season, each were fined $75 and taxed costs of $5.95. In default of payment, three months' terms in the county jail must be served. Disher was given 10 days in which to pay and Shomberg was allowed a few days time in which to attempt to secure the money.

Twenty-three trout, some of them a good size, 14 inches in length were confiscated by Browning. The officer reported that when he and Brooks came upon Disher and Shomberg, one was pounding the water with a long pole to frighten the fish into shallow water and the other was scooping the trout out with his hands. As trout are in headwaters of the ditches now, spawning, the fish are sluggish.

1928 – Bernard and family made the news again.

Stevens Point Daily Journal
January 16, 1928
BUENA VISTA FAMILY MOVES TO MILWAUKEE

Buena Vista, Wis. Jan 16------Mr. and Mrs. Bernard Shomberg and family of Buena Vista moved to 628 16th avenue, Milwaukee, on January 7. Mr. Shomberg and his family drove to Milwaukee in their car and Jacob and John Disher, sons of Lawrence Disher moved the furniture by truck. Mr. Shomberg is employed by Frank Deerdia, contractor and builder. His farm will be rented in the spring.

1930 On April 4th, 1930, Bernard Shomberg was 31 years old and lived at 560 16th Ave, Milwaukee, Wisconsin with his wife, Anna, son, 2 daughters and 4 boarders: Bernard and Joseph Waldoch, John Disher and Edward Schultz.

Bernard rented his home for $20.00. He worked as carpenter for the Electric Company

82	560	66	98	Shomberg, Bernard	Head	R	20
83				— Anna	Wife - H		
84				— Lorraine	Daughter		
85				— John	Son		
86				— Irene	Daughter		
87				Walldoch, Bernard	Boarder		
88				— Joseph	Boarder		
89				Disher, John	Boarder		
90				Schultz, Edward	Boarder		

1930 United States Federal Census.

NOTE: Today their address correspond to the Library of the Marquette University.

1940 – The 1940 Census provides us with much more information than the previous Censuses.

By April 28, 1940, Bernard Shomberg was 41 years old and owned his home, valued at $900.00. He lived in Stockton, Wisconsin with his wife, Anna, 4 sons, and 3 daughters. He had a 6th grade education, was a carpenter and worked 48 hrs a week, 52 weeks a year for $800.00.

His wife Anna was 36 yrs old, a homemaker, also with a 6th grade education and was the one answering the census taker. One interesting fact was that the 16 yrs old daughter Lorraine, was here named Valeria? I am assuming that it is Lorraine as she was born in the same year, 1924. Valeria/Lorraine had completed the 8th grade, since March 1st, 1940. The other children; John was 13 yrs old and had completed 6th grade, Irene was 10 yrs old and had completed 3rd grade and Bernard Jr was 8 yrs old and completed 2nd grade.

73						—, Harley	son	m	w	8	S	
74	...	30	O	900	yes	Shomberg, Bernard	Head	m	w	41	m	
75						—, Anna	wife	7	w	36	m	
76						— Valeria	daughter	7	w	16	S	
77	...					—, John	son	m	w	13	S	
78						—, Irene	daughter	7	w	10	S	
79						—, Vincent	son	m	w	8	S	
80						—, Theresa	daughter	7	w	4	S	

SUPPLEMENTARY QUESTIONS
For Persons Enumerated on Lines 46 and 80

Anton and Joseph are listed in the next page

ERSONS OF ALL AGES

PLACE OF BIRTH OF FATHER AND MOTHER

MOTHER TONGUE (OR LANGUAGE)

1940 United States Federal Census

1947 – Auction at the Shomberg's Farm

Wisconsin Rapids Daily Tribune – Saturday, July 5, 1947

Clintonville Sales Corp.

AUCTION

on the farm of

Bernard Shomberg

Known as the Frank Novotny or Yetter farm, located 7 miles southwest of Stevens Point or about 18 miles northeast of Wisconsin Rapids. ½ mile south of Stevens Point on County Trunk C, then south on County Trunk P to Linwood Town Hall, then south and west across Mill Creek bridge, then second farm on the left.

Having other business and employment we are selling our fine farm and personal property.

SATURDAY, July 12

SALE STARTS AT 12:30 P. M. SHARP

FARM

Consists of 140 acres of sand and clay loam soil, with about 80 acres cleared and 25 acres of good standing timber.

GROWING CROPS

15 acres of hay, 2 acres of potatoes, 6 acres of corn, 3 acres of beans, 2 acres of cucumbers, balance in pasture land.

BUILDINGS

7 room moden house with basement and furnace, newly remodeled, built-in cupboards, 34x50 ft. full basement, concreted barn with steel stalls and stanchions. Excellent 16x26 ft. concrete and stave silo, 12x24 ft. poultry house, 12x18 granary, 12x24 ft. double garage, 20x34 ft. wood shed, 12x24 ft. milk house, 6x8 ft. pump house. All buildings in good repair and fully electrified.

This farm is located on the high banks of the famous Wisconsin river, one of the beauty spots of the river. At this particular point there are beautiful islands, the best of fishing—ideal for a real resort. It is difficult to find words to fully express the beauty and the beauty that can be made with small cost. One must see this to appreciate it.

This farm will be sold in several parcels for cottages or altogether, whichever brings the highest price. Farm will be sold at 1:30 and can be bought on liberal terms.

LIVESTOCK

11 head of choice Holstein and Guernsey cattle, of which 7 are milk cows, 6 recently fresh, 1 to freshen soon. Holstein bull, 15 months old. Small Guernsey bull, 2 heifers. This herd shows very good production.

1 brood sow with 11 pigs, 3 feeder pigs weighing about 100 lbs. each, 100 heavy mixed spring pullets, and 2 Muscovy ducks.

FARM MACHINERY

Row crop tractor on rubber, new motor installed; 12-in. 2-bottom tractor plow; grain binder; sulky cultivator; grain seeder; disc harrow; mower; dump rake; spring tooth drag; sleigh; wagon on steel with rack; manure spreader; feed grinder; 1 single unit Delaval milking machine, cream separator, 5 milk cans, and many other small farm tools too numerous to mention.

BERNARD SHOMBERG, Owner

TERMS ON PERSONAL PROPERTY: All sums of $10.00 and under, cash, and above that amount one-fourth down and the balance in monthly payments.

Sale Conducted by:
Clintonville Sales Corp., Clintonville, Wis., Phone 289
Auctioneer: Adam Schider, Manawa, Wis.

1949 – Bernard and Anna visiting John Victor in Kentucky

1957 - US City Directories

Madison, Wisconsin, City Directory, 1957

HOMES
INCOME
PROPERTY
 	
—
 	
FARMS
 	
—
 	
BUSINESS
	--Jane A with UofW r Appleton Wis
	--Ralph W jr with U of W r Oregon, Wis
	Shomberg Anthony M USAF r139 S Hancock
	--Bernard C (Anna M) cabt mkr Paramount Builders
	   h139 S Hancock
	--David W with U of W r Bangor, Wis
	--John V (Yvonne M) carp Paramount Bldg h5818
	   Tolman ter
	--Theresa studt h139 S Hancock
	Shopette (John S Roth) gift shop 1115 N Sherman av

1964 Wisconsin State Journal April 7, 1964 – Building Permit for Shomberg Builders.

PAGE 6, SECTION 1   Building Permits

Records

CONTAGIOUS DISEASES	On Hand	New Cases	Re-leases	Re-maining
Chicken pox	20	25	9	36
German measles	21	37	12	46
Measles	6	0	0	6
Mumps	6	4	1	9
Scarlet fever	2	0	1	1
Strep throat	5	3	0	8
Whopping cough	0	5	0	5

Landfall dr., $18,000.

Robert Elsner, garage at 1610 National ave., $1,600.

Northland Manor Development Corp., houses at 918 Monica lane, 1017 Debra lane, and 4809 Ilene lane, $11,500 each.

Shomberg Builders, four-apartment building at 4710 Jenewein rd., $30,000, and house at 141 Nautilus dr., $18,300.

Dohm Construction Co., house at 1843 Waukesha st., $18,000

1970 – Bernard died on March 3rd, 1970.

The Daily Tribune Wisconsin Rapids. Saturday, March 7, 1970

in years.
bl
at

Bernard Shomberg

Funeral services were held in Madison this morning for Bernard C. Shomberg, 72, a resident of that city for 17 years and formerly of Stevens Point.

He was the father of Mrs. Lawrence Lange, 2940 Deer Rd., and is survived by his wife, four sons, three daughters, a brother and four sisters.

n,
it,
ie
d-
it-

a
r,
id
--

The Capital Times, Thursday, March 5th, 1970

30--THE.CAPITAL TIMES, Thursday, Mar. 5.1970

| — **Obituaries** —

Oh Saturday Morning
Rites for Bernard Shomberg, Retired Carpenter, Scheduled

Funeral services for Bernard C. Shomberg, 72, of 109 N. Firs St., retired carpenter, who diec Tuesday, will' be held Saturday at 10:30 a.m. in the Schroeder Funeral Home, 3325 E. Wash mgton Ave. Friends may call there after 3 Friday.

Burial will be in Sunset Memory Gardens Cemetery.

He was a member of the Calvary Gospel Church and the Carpenters and Joiners Local 314.

Surviving are his wife, Annafour, sons, John V., 5716 Arbor Vitae Pl.; Bernard J., 6118 Old Middleton Rd.; Anthony M., 109 N. ;First St.; and Joseph M., Sun Prairie; three daughters, Mrs. Lorraine Buelow, Wausau; Mrs. I r e n e Lang, Wisconsin Rapids; and Mrs. Theresa De Merchant, Manaus, Brazil; a brother, Sylvester, Milwaukee four s i s t e r s , Mrs. Theresa Kwapick, Duluth; Mrs. Faye Ressler and Mrs. Myra Hansen both of Stevens Point; and Mrs Wanda Walker, Golden Valley N.D., and 18 grandchildren

Bernard C. Shomberg

Burial place.

JOHN VICTOR SHOMBERG

When JOHN VICTOR SHOMBERG was born on August 29, 1926, in Milwaukee, Wisconsin, his father, BERNARD, was 29 and his mother, ANNA, was 23. He married YVONNE MARIE BENTLE on January 12, 1951, in Stevens Point, Wisconsin. They had six children in 11 years.

1.   Lynn M. Shomberg/DeMaria -1951

2.   John Gordon Shomberg/Ronilda P Sousa– 1952

3.   Leigh Anne Shomberg/Johnson – 1953

4.   James Jay Shomberg/Judith L Campbell – 1955

5.   Jay Allen Shomberg/Cynthia R Pirkl – 1959

6.   Joel Jeffrey Shomberg/Ginger L Clark - 1962

Timeline for JOHN VICTOR SHOMBERG

1930

In April 4th, 1930, John Shomberg was 3 years and 7/12 months old and lived at 16th Ave, Milwaukee, Wisconsin with his father, mother, and 2 sisters.

82	560	66	98	Shomberg, Bernard	Head	R	20
83				— Anna	Wife - H		
84				— Lorraine	Daughter		
85				— John	Son		
86				— Irene	Daughter		
87				Walldoch, Bernard	Boarder		
88				— Joseph	Boarder		
89				Nisher John	Boarder		
90				Schultz, Edward	Boarder		

1930 United States Federal Census

April 1, 1940

On April 1, 1940, John Shomberg was 13 years old, had finished 6th grade and lived in Stockton, Wisconsin with his father, mother, 3 brothers, and 3 sisters.

					— Harley	son	m	w	8	S	yes	1		Wisconsin		
30	O	900	yes	Shomberg, Bernard	Head	m	w	41	m	no	6		Wisconsin		Sc
				— Anna	wife	7	w	36	m	no	6		Wisconsin		Bc
				— Valeria	daughter	7	w	16	S	no	8		Wisconsin		Sc
				— John	son	m	w	13	S	yes	6		Wisconsin		Bc
				— Irene	daughter	7	w	10	S	yes	8		Wisconsin		Q
				— Vincent	son	m	w	8	S	yes	2		Wisconsin		Sc
				— Theresa	daughter	7	w	4	S	no	—		Wisconsin		

UPPLEMENTARY QUESTIONS — FOR PERSONS OF ALL AGES

1940 United States Federal Census

1949

On May 29th 1949 at 23 yrs old, he joined the Army at his Local Board #58, Stevens Point City, Portage, Wisconsin. He was a Private. He had blue eyes, brown hair, weighted 16 pounds and measured 5'8".

From April 5th to June 6th, 1949 he attended Leadership training at Fort Knox, 3rd Armed Division.

His duty assignment was 531st Quartermaster Petrol Supply Co

on 1/20/1950 was released from Fort Bragg, NC to the Army Reserve. HONORABLE discharge

FORCE: ATTACH TO SERVICE RECORD.
)NNEL. WASHINGTON. D.C

John Victor's signature

CHARACTER OF SEPARATION	REPORT OF SEPARATION FROM THE	DEPARTMENT
HONORABLE	ARMED FORCES OF THE UNITED STATES	ARMY

SEPARATION DATA

1. LAST NAME—FIRST NAME—MIDDLE NAME: Shomberg John Victor
2. SERVICE NUMBER: US55 005 775
3. GRADE—RATE—RANK AND DATE OF APPOINTMENT: Prt - 20 May 49 AUS
4. COMPONENT OR BRANCH OR

5. QUALIFICATIONS

SPECIALTY NUMBER OR SYMBOL: 0566
RELATED CIVILIAN OCCUPATION AND D.O.T. NUMBER: None
6. EFFECTIVE DATE OF SEPARATION: DAY 20 MONTH Jan YEAR 50
7. TYPE OF SEPARATION: Transfer to ERC

8. REASON AND AUTHORITY FOR SEPARATION: ETS Release to Reserve Component (SR 615-363-5)
9. PLACE OF SEPARATION: Fort Bragg, North Carolina

10. DATE OF BIRTH: DAY 29 MONTH Aug YEAR 26
11. PLACE OF BIRTH: Milwaukee, Wisconsin
12. DESCRIPTION: SEX Male | HAIR White | COLOR HAIR Brown | COLOR EYES Blue | HEIGHT 5'8" | WEIGHT 165

13. REGISTERED: X
14. SELECTIVE SERVICE NUMBER: 47 58 26 189
15. SELECTIVE SERVICE LOCAL BOARD NUMBER: Local Board #58, Stevens Point, Portage Co., Wisconsin
16. INDUCTED: DAY 21 MONTH Jan YEAR 49

17. ENLISTED IN OR TRANSFERRED TO A RESERVE COMPONENT: YES __ NO X

MEANS OF ENTRY OTHER THAN BY INDUCTION: Not applicable
ENLISTED __ REENLISTED __ COMMISSIONED __ CALLED FROM INACTIVE DUTY __
INTO ACTIVE SERVICE: Recruit

18. DATE AND PLACE OF ENTRY INTO ACTIVE SERVICE: MONTH Jan YEAR 49 PLACE Stevens Point, Wisc.
HOME ADDRESS AT TIME OF ENTRY INTO ACTIVE SERVICE: 126 Warner St., Stevens Point, Wisconsin, Portage County

SERVICE DATA

STATEMENT OF SERVICE FOR PAY PURPOSES | A YEARS | B MONTHS | C DAYS | ENLISTMENT ALLOWANCE PAID ON EXTENSION OR ENLISTMENT IF ANY: None

NET: Service completed for pay purposes excluding this period — Not applicable
NET SERVICE COMPLETED FOR PAY PURPOSES THIS PERIOD: 1 | 0 | 0
OTHER SERVICE (Act of 16 June 1942 as amended) COMPLETED FOR PAY PURPOSES: None
TOTAL NET SERVICE COMPLETED FOR PAY PURPOSES: 1 | 0 | 0

FOREIGN AND/OR SEA SERVICE: YEARS | MONTHS | DAYS — NO FOREIGN SERVICE

DECORATIONS, MEDALS, BADGES, COMMENDATIONS, CITATIONS AND CAMPAIGN RIBBONS AWARDED OR AUTHORIZED: None

MOST SIGNIFICANT DUTY ASSIGNMENT: 531st Quartermaster Petrl Supply Company

WOUNDS RECEIVED AS A RESULT OF ACTION WITH ENEMY FORCES: None

SERVICE SCHOOLS OR COLLEGES, COLLEGE TRAINING COURSES AND/OR POST-GRAD. COURSES SUCCESSFULLY COMPLETED	DATES From/To	MAJOR COURSE	SERVICE TRAINING COURSES SUCCESSFULLY COMPLETED
Fort Knox, Kentucky, 3rd Armd. Division	5 Apr-6 Jun 49	Leadership's	None

INSURANCE DATA

GOVERNMENT INSURANCE INFORMATION...

KIND OF INSURANCE: $10,000-$6.60 | N.S.L.I. | PREMIUM: NEGLI
MONTH ALLOTMENT DISCONTINUED: 31 January 1950
MONTH NEXT PREMIUM DUE: 28 February 1950
TRAVEL OR MILEAGE ALLOWANCE INCLUDED IN TOTAL PAYMENT: None
DISBURSING OFFICER'S NAME AND SYMBOL NUMBER: C. L. JOHNSON Major., FD 215-291

AUTHENTICATION

REMARKS: No time lost under AR 107
Blood Group "A"

SIGNATURE OF OFFICER AUTHORIZED TO SIGN
NAME, GRADE AND TITLE: ROLLIN K. LOCKS, 1st Lt.
Personnel Officer

PERSONAL DATA

V.A. BENEFITS PREVIOUSLY APPLIED FOR: None
COMPENSATION PENSION INSURANCE BENEFITS ETC
CLAIM NUMBER:

DATE OF LAST CIVILIAN EMPLOYMENT: FROM 1941 TO 1949
MAIN CIVILIAN OCCUPATION: Chauffeur
NAME AND ADDRESS OF LAST CIVILIAN EMPLOYER: VETS Cab Company, Stevens Point, Wisconsin.

UNITED STATES CITIZEN: YES X NO __
NON-SERVICE EDUCATION: GRAM. SCHOOL __ HIGH SCHOOL X COL./LEGE __ DEGREE(S) __
MAJOR COURSE OR FIELD:

MARITAL STATUS: Single | 3 | 0 | 0 | None
SIGNATURE OF PERSON BEING SEPARATED: John Victor Shomberg

PERMANENT ADDRESS FOR MAILING PURPOSES: 218 Dixon St., Stevens Point, Portage Co., Wisc.

DD FORM 214 | 1 JAN 50

HEADQUARTERS COPY (ARMY & AIR FORCE, ATTACH TO SERVICE RECORD
NAVY: TO BUREAU OF NAVAL PERSONNEL, WASHINGTON, D.C.
MARINE CORPS: AFFIXED TO SERVICE RECORD BOOK
COAST GUARD: TO HQ, COAST GUARD, WASHINGTON, D.C.)
2

Report of Separation DD-214

Quartermaster Corps Branch Insignia

1951 Marriage Certificate

John Victor and Yvonne were married at Tabernacle Parsonage, Stevens Point, WI by Reverend Marshall Schroeder. Lester Buelow and Lorraine Shomberg served as witnesses. At the time, John was 24 yrs old, was a cab driver and lived at 218 Dixon St, Stevens Point, WI. Yvonne was 20 yrs old and worked as a Comptometer Operator (comptometer was the first commercially successful key-driven mechanical calculator). She lived at 236 S. Illinois Ave, Stevens Point, WI.

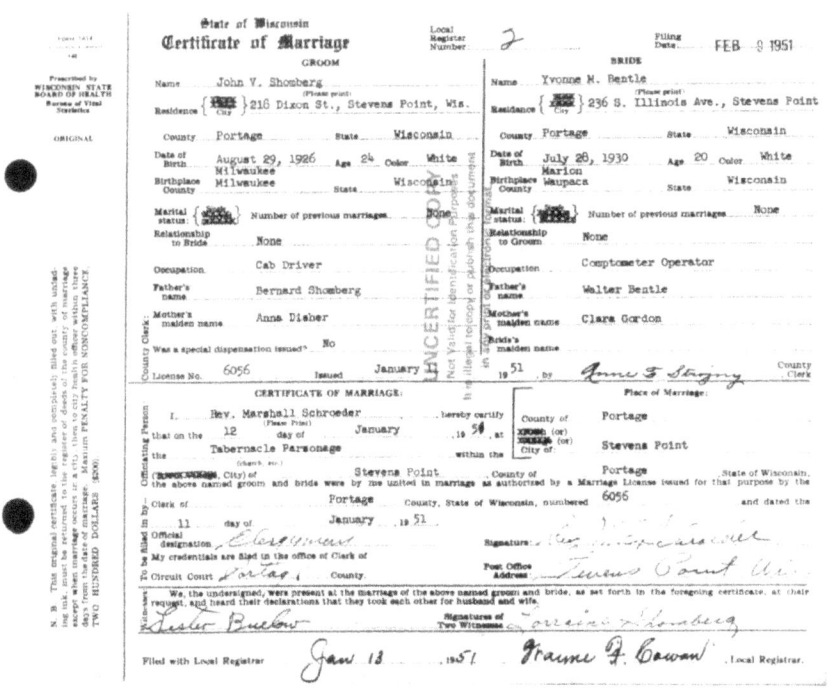

See Yvonne Bentle's family line in Volume 2

1957

U.S. City Directories, 1821-1989

Residence 1957: 5818 Tolman Terrace. Madison, Wisconsin, USA.
Carpenter at Paramount Builders. He worked at the same place where his
father Bernard was a cabinet maker.

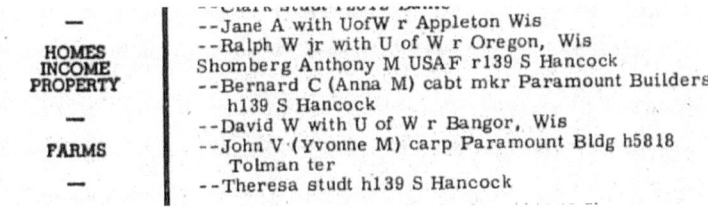

HOMES
INCOME
PROPERTY

FARMS

--Jane A with UofW r Appleton Wis
--Ralph W jr with U of W r Oregon, Wis
Shomberg Anthony M USAF r139 S Hancock
--Bernard C (Anna M) cabt mkr Paramount Builders
    h139 S Hancock
--David W with U of W r Bangor, Wis
--John V (Yvonne M) carp Paramount Bldg h5818
    Tolman ter
--Theresa studt h139 S Hancock

1974

John Victor and mother in law Clara Bentle

1982

US Public Records Index

Phone Number: 783-7696 Address: 1055 Laws Ci, Mazomanie, WI, 53560 (from 1982 to 1996) He also lived at 5744 Broadmore St, Zephyrhills, FL, 33542-3239

John Victor died on May 17, 1997, in Pasco Co., Florida, at the age of 70.

1997
The Tampa Tribune
Tuesday, May 20, 1997
Obituary

Deceased Name: JOHN VICTOR SHOMBERG

JOHN VICTOR SHOMBERG, 70 of Zephyrhills died Saturday at East Pasco Medical Center. He moved to this area eight years ago from Mazomanie, Wis. He was a retired carpenter, and an Army veteran of Korea War. He is survived by his wife Yvonne; four sons, John of Montgomery, Ala., James and Joel both of Mazomanie, and Jay of Sun Prairie, Wis.; two daughters Lynn DiMaria of Knoxville, Tenn., and Leigh Ann Johnson of Phoenix; and 12 grandchildren. Oakley Funeral Home, Zephyrhills

Burial: 20 May 1997, Sunset Memorial Gardens, Zephyrhills, Pasco County, FL.

Burial

Sunset Memory Gardens
Tampa, Hillsborough County, Florida, USA

5. THE DOMASZEKS

JOHN (JAN) DOMASZEK was born about 1815 in Poland. He married **CATHERINE SZULT** about 1835. He had four children by the time he was 28. He died about 1870 at the age of 55. CATHERINE was born about 1815 in Poland. She died about 1868.

They had 4 children:

1.   <u>THADDEUS DOMASZEK</u>   1836 – 1910

2.   Jan Domaszek Jr. - November 21, 1838 – June 27, 1924. Married to Katarzyna Josephine Piotrowski. Jan was buried at Sacred Heart Cemetery, Polonia, Portage County Wisconsin, USA Plot: F
They had 4 children:
        John L Domaszek 1865 – 1942
        Charles Domaszek 1871 – 1972 born in Wisconsin.
        Frances Domazek/Joseph Trzebiatouski 1876 – 1953
        Matthew Domaszek 1881 – 1952 born in Wisconsin

3.   Peter Domaszek – January 10, 1840 – March 12, 1912. Peter arrived in 1870, per 1900 Census. The Census also shows that he lived in Pike Lake, Marathon, Wisconsin, was the head of the household, married for 20 years to Augusta? but shows no other person with him.

4.   Mathias Domaszek - 1843 – July 18, 1924 in Stevens Point, Portage County, WI. No other records available.

THADDEUS DOMASZEK

When THADDEUS DOMASZEK was born on September 24, 1836, in Germany, his father, JOHN, was 21 and his mother, CATHERINE, was also 21. He was married three times and had seven sons and six daughters. He died on December 24, 1910, in Hull, Wisconsin, at the age of 74.

July 9, 1863

Thaddaus Damasche (sic) arrived in New York, New York, on July 9, 1863, at the age of 26. He came with his wife Paulina.

New York, Passenger Lists, 1820-1957

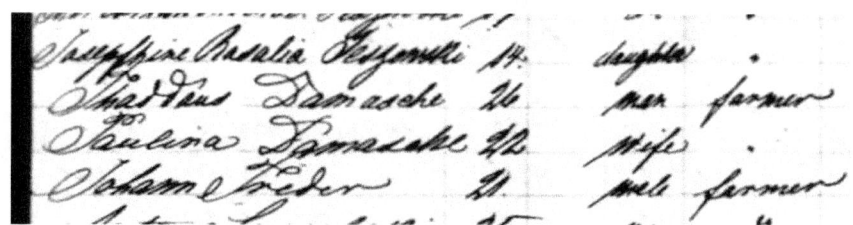

He was married to Paulina Marianna Marchel. They had 3 children.

Peter Domaszek – no records

Mary C Domaszek – 1866-1943

Joseph Domaszek – 1870

1871 Marriage to MARIANNA She was born in 1843 (Other possible names: Marianna Cera or Cyran or Cyra per Our Family History by Myron M. Felckowski. Family tree database updated March 25, 2013. Families of Portage County, Wisconsin). She died in 1889 in Hull, Portage, WI (tombstone says "Mother Mary" but it was common for names to be shortened (Americanized). They had seven children:

1. Thaddeus Domaszek Jr 1872 – 1952 no other records

2. <u>FRANCES BRONYSTAWA DOMASZEK</u> 1876 – 1936

3. Frank Domaszek 1876 – 1947 no other records

4. Julianna Domaszek/Behling 1881 – 1957
    They had children:
        Helen Behling
        Myron Behling - ? – 1918
        Edward Behling - 1911 – ?
        Edna Behling - 1913 – ?
        James Fravie Behling 1915 – 1993
        Charles Behling 1916 – 1990
        Melven Behling 1918 – 1993
        Josephine Behling 1921 – ?

5. Anna Rosa Domaszek/Jankowski 1885 – ?
    They had 9 children:
        Josephine Jankowski 1899 – ?
        Frank Jankowski 1902 – ?
        John Edward Jankowski 1906 – 1993
        Dorota Rozalia Jankowski 1907 – 1920
        Isabel Jankowski 1909 – ?
        Irene Jankowski 1911 – ?
        Thaddius Jankowski 1912 – ?
        Catherine Jankowski 1914 – ?
        Florence Jankowski 1917 – ?

6. Anton Domaszek 1888 – ? No other records

7. Stanislaus Domaszek 1888 – 1895 No other records

1895   Thomas Domaszek lived in Hull, Wisconsin in 1895.

U.S., Indexed County Land Ownership Maps, 1860-1918

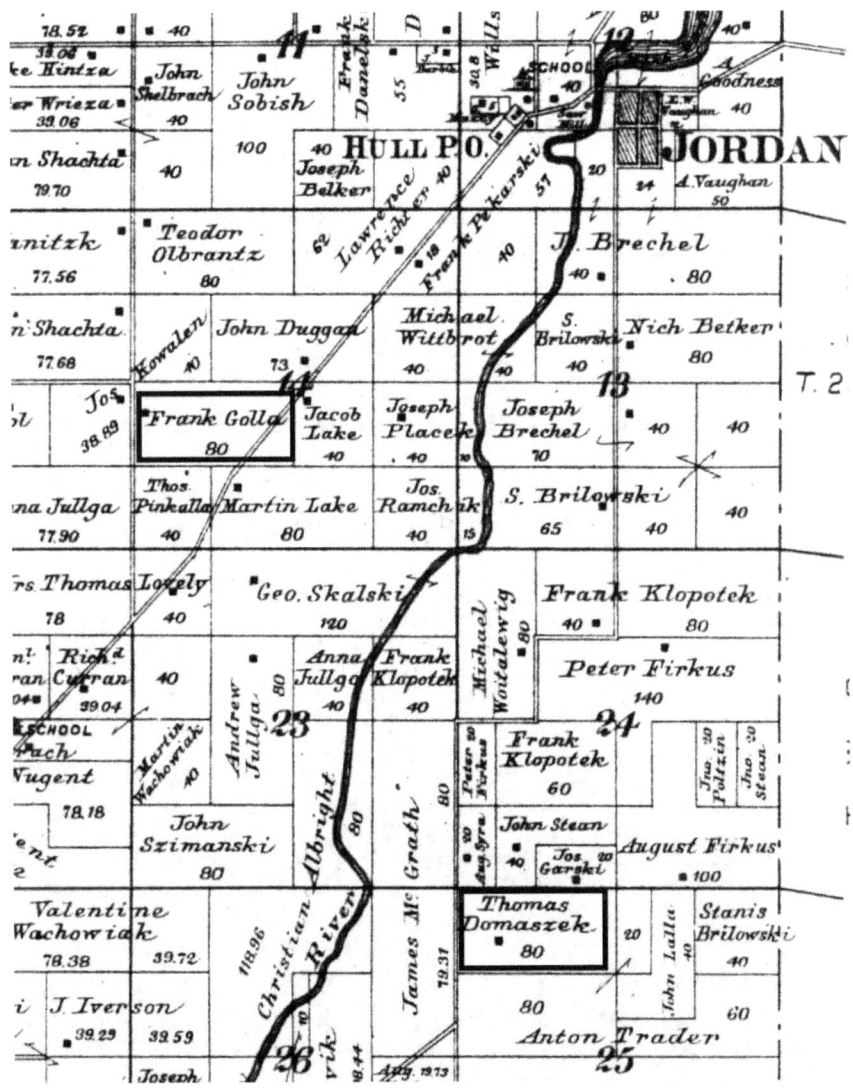

Note Frank Golla's land above left from Thaddeus. Thaddeus later married his widow Frances.

1900

Thadeus Damask (sic) married Frances (Francisca Kaszer) Dominick Golla in 1890. She was born in 1854 in Prussia Poland. She died on 15 May 1924 in Hull, Portage, WI (Info from book Golla Relatives History at Portage County Public Library Compiled by Agnes Kawleski-Golla before 12 Nov 1994).

They had three children in 12 years.
Martha Domaszek 1891 – 1983

Cecilia Domaszek 1893 – 1963

Thadeus Damasche 1896 –

In June 2nd, 1900, he was 64 years old and lived in Hull, Wisconsin with his wife, Frances, 5 sons, and 3 daughters. Two of the sons were step-sons: Leo Domasek 19 yrs old and Anton Domasek 18 yrs old. The twins Anton and Stanislaus 16 yrs old and Rosa 15 yrs old (Marianna sons and daughter) and Thaddeus and Frances 2 daughters and son; Martha, Cecilia and Thaddeus. Thaddeus rented his home, could not read or write but spoke English.

1900 United States Federal Census

June 1, 1905

On June 1, 1905, Tadush (sic) Domasek was 78 years old and lived in Hull, Wisconsin with his wife, Francis, 2 stepsons, 3 sons, and 2 daughters. All of the ones listed in 1900 minus Rosa.

Wisconsin, State Censuses, 1895 and 1905

1910

The April 17, 1910 Census says that he was a farmer, own his home with mortgage, spoke Polish and could not read or write. He lived on Brachel Road (Town of Hull) with his wife Francis, daughter Martha, sons Anthony (Anton?), Steve (Stanislaus) and Thaddeus, and stepson Anton Golla.

1910 United States Federal Census Page 1

Page 2 - note that they have a 67 yrs old servant named Josephine.

1910 Thaddeus died on December 24 and was buried on December 27th in St Peter's Cemetery, Stevens Point, Portage, WI.

> **Note:** Section 2: Mary (1843-1889) and Thaddeus Damaszek (1836-1910). From:[PortageCoWI Cemetery Photos]

FRANCES BRONYSTAWA DOMASZEK

When FRANCES BRONYSTAWA DOMASZEK was born on October 3, 1876, in Wisconsin, her father, THADDEUS, was 40 and her mother, MARIANNA, was 33. She married JOSEPH FRANK SHOMBERG on January 12, 1891, in Sharon, Wisconsin. They had 14 children in 21 years. She died on August 16, 1936, in Stevens Point, Wisconsin, at the age of 59.

1921 September 24th - divorce from Joseph Shomberg

DIVORCE DECREE IS SET ASIDE BY JUDGE

Stevens Point—Frances Shomberg and Joseph F. Shomberg, city, who on September 24, 1921, were divorced in circuit court here, have become reconciled and today a judgment was entered setting aside the verdict. The judgment was entered at their petition.

1927

Frances Shomberg lived in Stevens Point, Wisconsin at house number 160 Superior Ave, her daughter Mary lived with her. She is a bit upset, as we can see that she claims to be the widow of Jos F, listed below her name, with the wife Anna.

U.S. City Directories, 1821-1989

Shomberg Frances (wid Jos F) h160 Superior av
Shomberg Jos F (Anna) lab h125 Hardig av
Shomberg Mary student r160 Superior av
Shopinski Frank beatermn Whiting-Plover Paper Co r
  RD 5

1930

On April 21st, 1930, Frances Shomberg was 53 years old, divorced and lived at Superior Ave in Stevens Point, Wisconsin with her 13 yrs old son, Sylvester. She owns her home valued at $1,200.00 and does not own a radio set. She did not attended school but is able to read and write. She was a servant for a private family and her son was a newsboy working in the streets.

1930 United States Federal Census

1936 Frances died August 16, 1936 and was laid to rest at her father's family plot in St Peter's Cemetery, Hull, WI

1936 – She was buried on August 20, 1936. St Peter's Cemetery Section 2 _ grave inscription: Shomberg Frances [nee Damask] [16 Nov] 1876-[16 Aug] 1936.

6. THE DISHERS

FRANZ DISHER was born in 1826 in the Village of Podjass German-Poland (Podjazy in Polish). He married MARIANNA ANNA WOSNIK about 1844. They had one child (of record) during their marriage.

JACOB PHILIPP DISHER was born April 30, 1846 in Podjazy, District of Kartuzy, Glansk Province, Poland, and died December 1, 1931 in Plover, WI. He married EMILIA DOMBROWSKI February 8, 1870 in Village of Suleczyno Catholic Church, District of Kartuzy, Gdansk Province, Poland, daughter of AUGUSTIN DOMBROWSKI and ANTONINA VON KLOPOTEK. She was born April 14, 1844 in Village of Borek, District of Karthaus, Province of Gdansk, Poland, and died May 9, 1918 in Plover, WI.

See Emilia's family line in Chapter #7

1848 April 30th – Birth of Jacob.

Note for Jacob's birth: Naturalization papers says born abt 1844---1900 Census says born May 1846---January 1920 Census says age 74 last bday - 1845---family history says 1848---Disher online says 1846 and 1848 (see below)

1848 – Baptism
Family history library microfilm 30.072.747. Entry #25 shows the birth of Jacob to Franz Discher & Marianna Anna Wosnik on April 30, 1848, in

the village of Podjazy/Podjass. The child was baptized on May 3, 1848 at the Suleczyno Catholic Church. Baptized on May 3rd. The name of the father is Franz. The mother of Jacob Philipp was Marianna Anna Wosnik and the godparents were Franz Maikowski and Constancia Wieczorek.

They all were from village Podjas which is today called Podjazy in parish Suleczyno.

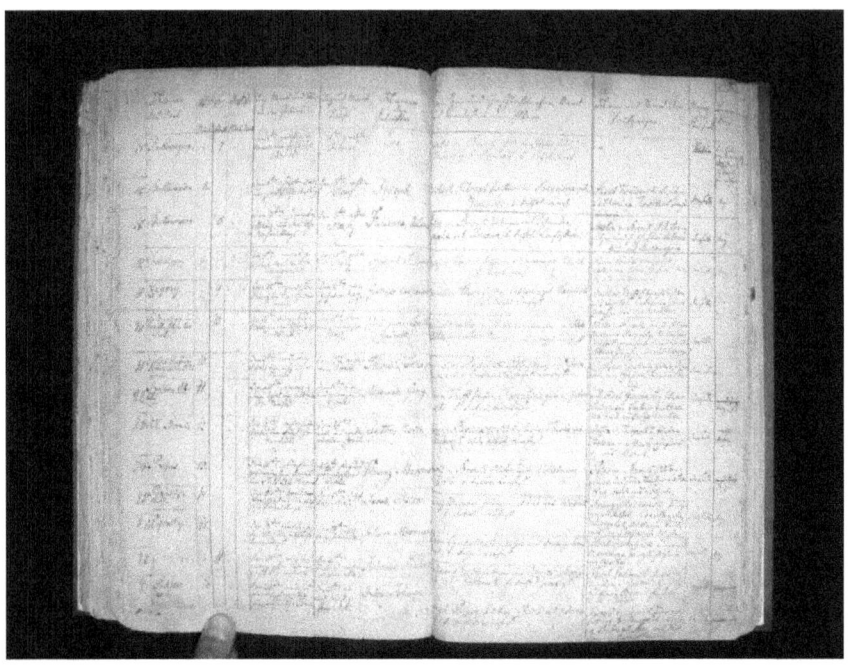

1867 – Jacob's Military service: November 1, 1867, joined the 6th Pomeranian Artillery Company.

1870 – Jacob and Emilie were married on February 8th. At the Village of Suleczyno Catholic Church, District of Kaszuby, Gdansk Province, Poland.

Suleczyno Holy Trinity Church (as seen today)

Village of Suleczyno, Poland (as seen today)

1881 – Jacob arrived on the Ship Oder on April 9,1881. His name is on page 352 left column 15 from the top and above him is his brother-in-law, Dombroska, August and his wife Pauline.

On the Microfilm from the ship's manifest he was number 291 and his brother-in-law and wife were 289 & 290 respectively.

[Broderbund Family Archive #356, Ed. 1, Germans to America, 1875-1888, Date of Import: Aug 5, 2005, Internal Ref. #1.356.1.9987.13]

Passenger's Name: Jacob Discher
Age: 36
Gender: Male
Occupation: None
Last Residence: Germany
Date of Arrival: Apr. 09, 1881
Final Destination: USA
Ship's Name: Oder
Manifest ID Number: 36021
Port of Embarkation: Bremen & Southampton

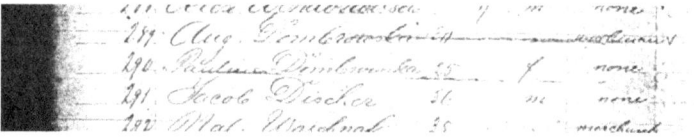

1881 - His wife Emilie and Children followed on the ship, ODER, arriving in New York on October 31, 1881 from Bremen.

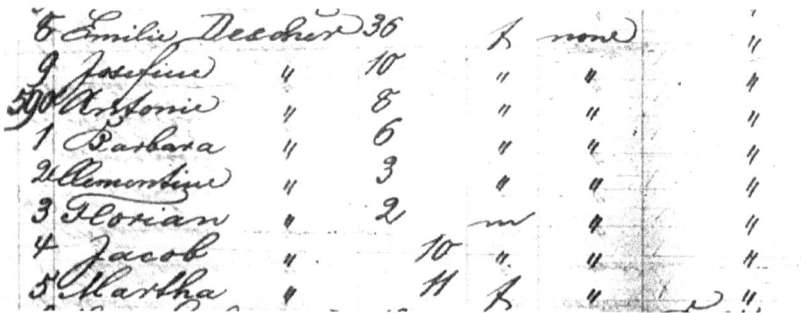

The information for Emilia (Dombrowski) Disher is located in a book Germans to America Lists of Passengers Arriving at U.S. Ports. Volume 40 (P74-4605 to find microfilm of ship manifest) Edited by Ira A. Glazier and P. William Filby

Emilie and the kids came on the same ship Oder but arriving on

October 31,1881

They are on page 416 middle of left column, spelled as Descher, Emilie and the children -- Josefine 10, Antonia 8, Barbara 6, Clementine 3, Florian 2, Jacob 10 months, and Martha 11 months.

On the Microfilm from the ship's manifest she is number 589 through 595 respectively.

The ages listed in the manifest for Florian, Martha and Jacob differ from the 1900 Census which list them as 22, 20 and 18 yrs old meaning that at their arrival Florian was 3, Martha was 1 and Jacob was not yet born?!

S.S. ODER, 1873 North German Lloyd
Courtesy The Peabody Museum of Salem

230

The picture of the ship is from a book. Ships of our Ancestors by Michael J. Anuta 1983

Page 230. SS Oder, 1873 North German Lloyd Menomonee, Michigan 49858-9775. Also Library of Congress Catalog Card # 83-91402

1900 – The 12th Census of the US, Enumerated on June 4th, 1900 listed their residence in Stockton, Portage, WI. Jacub (sic) Disher was 54 yrs old, with a date of birth of May 1846. He was born in Poland, Prussia

[Poland;Germany]. His Immigration Year was 1881. He was married to Amelia (sic) Disher since 1870. She was born in April 1844. Both Jacub's and Amelia's parents were born in Poland, Prussia.

His occupation is listed as farmer, he owns his farm and has a mortgage. He can read, write and speak English.

Other household members are: Lawrence Disher age 22, farm laborer, Martha Disher age 20, Jacub Disher 18, also a farm laborer and two new children born in Wisconsin, John Disher age 15 and Frank Disher age 14. Josephine, Antonia, Barbara and Clementine are no longer living at home.

1900 US Federal Census

1906 – Naturalization

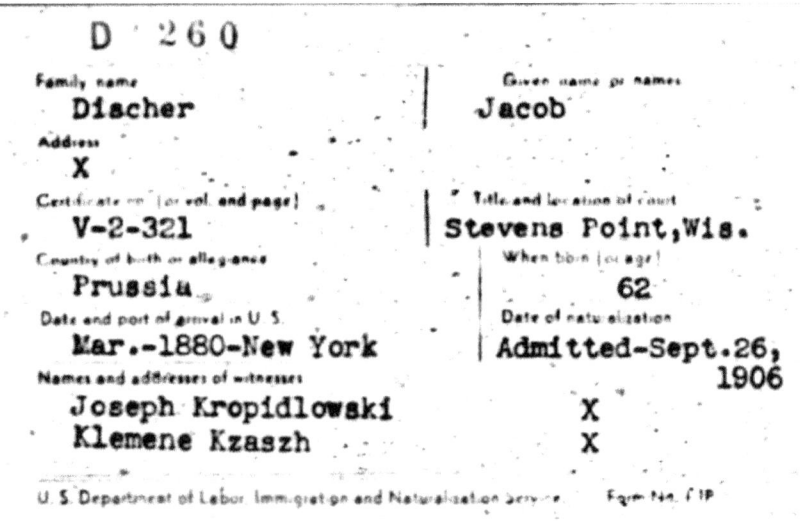

US Naturalization Record Indexes

Jacob became a naturalized citizen on 9/26/1906. Note the "c" added to Discher.

1910 – Jacob and Emilia Portrait

1915 – Portage County Atlas shows:

Disher, John, Farmer, S. 4, T. Grant, P. 0. Grand Rapids.

Disher, Lawrence, Farmer, S. 12, T. Grant, P. 0. Plover.

Dischler, Joe J., Farmer and Stock raiser, S. 22, T. Plover, P. 0. Stevens Point. Mr. Dischler was born in Germany in 1871 and came to Portage County in 1881.

In the news:

Plover Property Sold –

Leo Sczypior receives $600.00 for transfer of 2 lots to Jacob Disher. Leo Sczypior has sold lots 1,2 & 7,8 block #6, original plot of the Village of Plover to Jacob Disher The price was $600.00.

Homestead of Jacob and Emilia

Descendants of Jacob Disher
Family (Rodzina) portrait of Jakób i Emilija Dyszer

Standing

Clementina	Barbara	Martha	Jacob Jr.	Frank	John	Lawrence
Married	Married	Married	Married	Married	Married	**(Florian)**
August	John H	Michael	Pauline	Catherine	Matilda	Married
Okoniewski	Singer	Arbuch	Flisakowski	Dudzik	Skrzypkowski	Matilda
Michael						Ostrowski
Zblewski						
Nicholas						
Herrick						

Front Row

Antoinette	Emeilia Dombrowski	Jacob Sr. Discher	Joseph
Married	**Discher**		Married
Anthony			Stacia
Ksionsk			Mansavage

76

1915 – Jacob and Emilia Portrait

1920 – On January 2nd 1920, Jacob lived on Main Street, Plover Village, Portage, Wisconsin with his 17 yrs old granddaughter Agnes Okonuzski (probably daughter of Clementine and August Okoniewski)

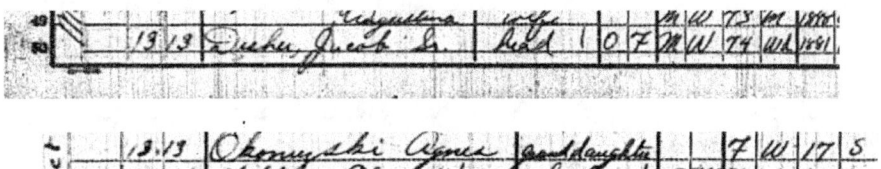

1920 United States Federal Census

1931 – December 5th
Stevens Point Daily Journal
Saturday, December 5, 1931
Obituary

JACOB DISHER, 85, DIES AT HIS HOME AT PLOVER TODAY

Jacob Disher, 85 a resident of Portage County for 50 years, died at noon today at his home at Plover. He was a retired farmer and had resided at Plover for the past 15 years.

Mr. Disher was born in Poland on April 30, 1856, and was married in that country. He and his family came to America when he was 35 years of age and located at once in the town of Stockton. They remained there for 35 years, and upon retiring 15 years ago Mr. Disher moved to Plover village with his family. His wife died on May 10, 1918.

He is survived by the following sons and daughters; Jacob Disher, Jr., of Stockton, John of the town of Grant, Frank of Stevens Point, Lawrence of Plover, Mrs. Anton Ksiansk of the town of Sharon, Mrs. Nick Herrick of Galloway, and Mrs. John Singer of the town of Grant; two other children preceded their father in death, Joe, who lived in Chicago, and Martha Arbush, Stevens Point. Mr. Disher is also survived by 48 grandchildren and 43 great-grandchildren.

The funeral will be held at 8:30 o'clock Tuesday morning at St. Mary's church at Fancher and burial will follow in the parish cemetery. The body will be taken to the Disher home at Plover this evening from the Paris funeral home.

Funeral of Mr. Disher
Stevens Point Daily Journal
December 7, 1931

Funeral services for Jacob Disher of Plover, pioneer resident of Portage county, who died at his home Saturday noon, were held at 9 o'clock Wednesday morning at St. Mary's church at Fancher. Many relatives and friends were present. Rev. S. Lapinski of Plover said a requiem mass at the main alter, while Rev. S. J. Kubiszewski gave a sermon and Father Lapinski officiated at the burial, which took place in the parish cemetery.

St. Stanislaus' society of St. Mary's church, of which Mr. Disher had been a member, attended the services in a body.

Pallbearers were four sons, and two sons-in-law of Mr. Disher, John, Frank, Florian, and Jacob Disher, Anton Ksiansk and John Singer.

St Mary of Mount Carmel Church

St. Mary's Cemetery, Fancher, Wisconsin, Portage County

Children of JACOB DISHER and EMILIA DOMBROWSKI are:

1.   Joseph Disher, b. April 1, 1871, Village of Tuchlin, District of Kartuzy, Gdansk Province, Poland; d. November 17, 1930, Chicago, Cook County IL.. He married Estacia (Annastazia) Mansavage. She was born in 1874 in Wisconsin, USA.
        They had one child:
              Joseph Disher 1912-1970

2.   Antonette Disher, b. July 28, 1872, Village of Tuchlin, District of

Kartuzy, Gdansk Province, Poland; d. September 28, 1944, Town of New Hope, WI.. She married Anthony Kszosk and they had 7 children:

> Annie Kszosk 1902 – ?
> Jacob Kszosk 1904 – ?
> Celia Kszosk 1906 – ?
> Josepe Kszosk 1908 – ?
> Mike Kszosk 1911 – ?
> Andrew Kszosk 1913 – ?
> Susan Kszosk 1917 – ?

3.   Barbara Disher, b. December 1st, 1873, Village of Cieszenie, District of Kartuzy, Gdansk Province, Poland; d. April 18, 1963, Portage County Infirmary, Whiting, Portage County, WI. On Feb. 6, 1891, she was married at St. Mary of Mt. Carmel Catholic Church, Fancher, to Mr. John H. Singer. They had 15 children, 30 grandchildren, 61 great-grandchildren and one great-great-grandchild.

> Frank B Singer 1893 – 1968
> Johanna Singer 1895 – 1989
> Genevieve M. Singer 1897 – 1954
> Genlatetta Jennie Singer 1897 –
> Susan Singer 1898 – 1978
> Francis Fiona Singer 1900 – 1983
> Regina E. Singer 1902 – 1973
> Martha Singer 1903 –
> Louis C. Singer 1905 – 1975
> Margaret Singer 1907 – 1996
> Leo T Singer 1909 – 1973
> Bernice Singer 1911 – 1986
> Henry N. Singer 1913 – 1982
> Belvina Dorothy Singer 1915 – 1994
> Katherine E. Singer 1918 – 1999

4.   Clementina Disher, b. November 23, 1875, Village of Cieszenie, District of Kartuzy, Gdansk Province, Poland; d. December 26, 1958, Stevens Point, Portage County, WI.. She was hurried there by ambulance after having been home for a week since a one month previous hospitalization. She was married on Jan. 23, 1899, to August Okoniewski at St. Mary of Mount Carmel Catholic Church at Fancher. They had 6 children:

> Mary Anna Okoniewski 1899 – 1988
> Peter Okoniewski 1901 – 1938
> Agnes S Okoniewski 1903 – 1984
> Magdalena Okoniewski 1905 – 1977

Steve I. Okoniewski 1907 – 1983
Franciszek Francis Okoniewski 1910 – 1910

5.   LAWRENCE (FLORIAN) DISHER, , b. January 7, 1878, Village of Cieszenie, District of Kartuzy, Gdansk Province, Poland; d. May 13, 1934, Town of Grant, Portage County, WI.

6.   Martha Disher, b. March 25, 1880, Village of Cieszenie, District of Kartuzy, Gdansk Province, Poland; d. March 11, 1916, at home, Stevens Point, Portage County, WI.. She married Michael Arbush on 12 May 1904 in Fancher, Wisconsin. He was 24 yrs older than her (and had seven children!) They had one child:
Joseph Disher Arbush 1912 – 1970

7.   Jacob Disher, b. January, 1881, Village of Cieszenie, District of Kartuzy, Gdansk Province, Poland; d. April 4, 1958, at Home, Stevens Point, Portage County, WI.. He married Pauline Flisakowski. She was born on 01 Jul 1883 in Góra Kalwaria, Mazowieckie, Poland. She died on 09 Oct 1968 in Stevens Point, Portage, Wisconsin, United States. They had 7 children:
Peter Disher 1905 – 1987
John Phillip Disher 1907 – 1971
Frank (Francis) Disher 1909 – 1980
Stanley Disher 1911 – 1988
Regina Disher 1913 – 2002
Mary A Disher 1915 – 2004
Raymond Disher 1917 – 1975

8.   John Disher, b. June 24, 1883, Town of Stockton, Portage County, WI.; d. May 4, 1956, St. Michael's Hospital, Stevens Point, Portage County, WI. He married Mathilda Martha Skryzphkowski. She was born on 25 Dec 1886 in Germany. She died on 10 Feb 1984 in Wisconsin, Marathon. They had 5 children:
Harry S Disher 1909 – 1983
Edward Disher 1914 – 1940
Sister Evelyn Disher 1915 – 2007
Leonard Disher 1917 – 1970
Bridget Leona Disher 1919 – 2005

9.   Frank Salszy Disher, b. January 20, 1885, Town of Stockton, Portage County, WI.; d. March 15, 1948, at Home, Stevens Point, Portage County, WI.. He married Katherine Dudzik on 04 May 1910 in Stevens Point City, Portage, Wisconsin (at St Peter's Church by Rev. A.S.Elbert). She was born

on 26 Feb 1889 in Jordan, Portage, Wisconsin, United States. She died on 11 Sep 1939 in Stevens Point, Portage, Wisconsin, United States. They had 4 children:

> Margaret Disher 1911 – 1969
> Evelyn Disher 1912 – 1995
> Edmund Disher 1915 – 1965
> Raymond James Disher 1920 – 2005

LAWRENCE DISHER

LAWRENCE (FLORIAN) DISHER was born January 7, 1878 in Village of Cieszenie, District of Kartuzy, Gdansk Province, Poland, and died May 13, 1934 in Town of Grant, Portage County, WI.. He married MATHILDA OSTROWSKI November 5, 1900 in St. Bronislva Catholic, Plover, Portage County, WI, daughter of LEON OSTROWSKI and FRANCES KIEDROWSKI. She was born February 28, 1882 in Alice(Ellis), WI, and died March 16, 1993 in Portage County Heath Care Center, Whiting, Portage County, WI..

See Mathilda's ancestors in Chapter #8

1878 - When LAWRENCE (FLORIAN) DISHER was born on January 7, 1878, in Gdansk, Poland, his father, JACOB, was 32 and his mother, EMILIA, was 33.

1881 – Lawrence arrived in America with his mother Emilia and siblings in the ship ODER from Bremen, Germany.

1900 - 4 Jun At the age of 22, Lawrence lived with his parents in the Town of Stockton, South Side, Portage, Wisconsin. The Census shows that he was Single, living at home, DOB Feb 1878; Born: Poland-Prussia; parents born same place; immigration:1881; Occupation: Farm Laborer and he can read, write and speak English.

1900 US Federal Census

1900 – In October 30th, Lawrence Disher sworn his intention to become an American Citizen and to renounce forever any allegiance...to the Emperor of Germany

1900 - 3 Nov at the age of 22 Lawrence applied for a marriage license, per Stevens Point Journal Announcement. Stevens Point City, Portage, Wisconsin

The Stevens Point Journal.

EDWARD McGLACHLIN, Editor and Proprietor.   Devoted to the interests of Central Wisconsin, and the Vindication of Republican Principles   TERMS---$2.00 per Annum

VOL. XXXII,---NO. 18.   STEVENS POINT, WIS., SATURDAY, NOVEMBER 3, 1900.   WHOLE NUMBER 2,547

Thomp-
the po-
plea of
d costs,
This he

of the unfortunate lady, spent a few days with her last week.

fine shot

About

Marriage Licenses.

Frank Dulek, Stockton; Victoria Palebk, Sharon.

Harry Ellis, Pine Grove; Abbie Rice, Belmont.

)eWitt's
urn and
vill cure
id ugly
ain cure
e offered
original
Taylor

Louis Zozki, Bessemer; Martha Hintz, Belmont.

Frank Rybicki, Alban; Mary Pawelsky, Sharon.

Frank Yack, Stevens Point; Stella Kryszak, Stevens Point.

Lawrence Dasher, Stockton, Matilda Ostrowski, Plover.

funeral of
field Thu
the 73d y
at Plainfi

J. M.
dent of
Marshfield
is known
that city
dent that
contempl
a part of

1900 - 5 Nov Lawrence's Marriage to MATHILDA OSTROWSKI at St. Bronislva Catholic Church, Plover, Portage County, WI

Lawrence and Mathilda had 10 children:

1.   Gertrude A Disher/Schlickting was born on 22 Apr 1902 in Wisconsin, USA. She died in Sep 1972 in Schofield, Marathon, Wisconsin, United States. She married Erving Schlickting in 1952.

2.   ANNA DISHER 1903 – 1973

3.   Katherine Florence Disher was born on 10 Feb 1905 in Stevens Point, Portage, Wisconsin. She died on 05 Jan 1998 in Valrico, Florida, Hillsborough County. She married Joseph F. Wiater on 22 Sep 1924 in Plover, Wisconsin, Portage County. He was born on 28 Feb 1895 in Chicago, Illinois, Cook County. He died on 21 Sep 1955 in Stevens Point, Wisconsin, Portage County. They had 2 children:
        Jeanette G. Wiater 1925 – 1990
        Donald Wiater 1927 – 1976

4.   Frances Disher was born on 14 Sep 1907 in Wisconsin Rapids, Wood, Wisconsin, United States. She died on 21 Feb 1984 in Stevens Point, Portage, Wisconsin, United States of America. She married Nicholas (Nick) Wasieleski on 14 Oct 1924 in Plover, Portage, Wisconsin, United States. He

was born on 28 Nov 1888 in Poland. He died on 22 Jul 1973 in Stevens Point, Portage, Wisconsin, United States. They had 5 children:

> Gladys Wasieleski 1925 – 2005
> Leonard W Wasieleski 1928 – 1992
> Dorothy A Wasieleski 1930 – 2000
> Leona E. "Leo" Wasieleski 1933 – 2003
> Nicholas "Nick" Wasieleski Jr 1940 – 2010

5.   Jacob Disher was born on November 9, 1909 in Wisconsin, USA. He died on 11 Dec 1969 in Milwaukee, Milwaukee, Wisconsin, United States. He married Helen Rakowski. They had 2 children but no records are available.

6.   Theodore B Disher was born on 29 May 1914 in Linwood, Portage, Wisconsin, United States. He died on 15 Apr 1979 in Marshfield, Wisconsin, Wood County. He married Agnes A Cisewski on 27 Nov 1934 in St. Peter's Catholic Church, Stevens Point, Wisconsin, Portage County. She was born on 30 Nov 1917 in Stevens Point, Wisconsin, Portage County. She died on 15 Mar 2008 in Stevens Point, Wisconsin, Portage County. They had 14 children:

> Charlotte Disher
> Conrad Disher/Patricia
> David Disher
> Donald Disher/Linda
> Florian Disher/Barbara
> Gerald Disher//Diane
> Geraldine Disher ? – 1943
> Margaret Disher/Woiak
> Patricia Disher/Humphry
> Ronald Disher/Delores
> Theodore Disher Jr. 1939 – 1941
> August Disher 1942 – 2012
> Betty Disher 1945 – 1974
> Elaine Ellen Disher 1959 – 1962

7.   Benjamin (Bennie) Disher was born on 14 May 1916 in Plover, Portage, Wisconsin, United States. He died on 20 Nov 1961 in Milwaukee, Milwaukee, Wisconsin, United States. No record of marriage or children.

9.   Aloise Joseph Disher was born on 02 Aug 1918 in Plover, Portage, Wisconsin, United States. He died on 07 Apr 1981 in Milwaukee, Milwaukee, Wisconsin, United States. He married Virginia Shulfer in 1942.

10.   Evelyn K Disher was born on 23 Mar 1921 in Grant, Portage, Wisconsin, United States. She died on 16 Dec 1968 in West Allis, Milwaukee, Wisconsin, United States. She married Anton O. Brathovde

Lawrence and Mathilda Portrait

1905 – Per Wisconsin State Census, in the last day of June at age 26 (born 1878), Lawrence resided with wife Mathilda and daughters Gertrude, Anna and Katherine, in the 4th Ward of the City of Stevens Point, Portage, Wisconsin. He was born in Poland-Germany; was a Cabinet Maker and owned his house with a mortgage.

1905 Wisconsin State Census

1906 - 27 Sep. Lawrence was 28 yrs old when his Naturalization was approved. Record 2 page 452, Court of Portage County, Wisconsin.

STATE OF WISCONSIN, ⎱ *ss.* I *Lawrence Discher* ....*do solemnly*
County of Portage, ⎰
swear, in the presence of Almighty God, that I will support the Constitution of the United States, and that I do absolutely and entirely renounce and abjure all allegiance and fidelity to every foreign Prince, Potentate, State or Sovereignty whatever, and more particularly the allegiance and . fidelity which I in anywise owe to

.....*Emperor of Germany*........... *whereof I was heretofore a citizen or subject.*

                                        Lawrence Discher

Subscribed and sworn to in open Court, this ..*27*.. *day of* ..*Sept*

.................................*A. D. 1906*

                                        J.H. Timm .... *Clerk.*

1910 Lawrence Portrait

Lawrence (Florian) Discher
taken about 1910
age about 35

1910 - 20 Apr. When he was 32 yrs old, Lawrence resided in Grand Rapids Ward 6, Wood, Wisconsin with his wife and 5 children; he has been married for 8 yrs; his Birth Place is listed as German Polish; he arrived in 1881; his occupation was that of laborer at a paper mill. He was able to read but not write. He owns home with mortgage and it was a house not farm. His 3 older children were attending school. Note that his age is shown as 32 yrs old hence born 1878.

1910 US Federal Census

1918 - 2 Nov. At the age of 42 (registration card shows DOB January 1876) Lawrence registered with the Military Portage, Wisconsin. He was of medium height, medium built, blue eyes and brown hair.

WWI Draft Registration Card #2421

1920 - 10 Jan. Lawrence was 43 yrs old. He resided in the Township of Grant, Portage, Wisconsin with his wife and children. Gertrude and Anna are no longer living at home but 4 more sons have been added to the household (John, Theodore, Benjamin and Alois), also son Jacob is now called Albert. He owns his home with mortgage. He arrived 1880; Naturalized 1910; Able to read but not write; he was born in Germany; his mother tongue is Polish; he was not able to speak English; he was a farmer, working on his own account.

1920 US Federal Census

1920 – January 9th. Same year census shows Anna (age 16) and Katharyn (age 14) living as servants in the household of Alda Gilda (keeper of a boarding home) at 340 Pine Street, 2nd Ward of the City Stevens Point.

1930 - 15 Apr. Lawrence and his family (a new daughter Evelyn has been added) reside in the town of Grant, Portage, Wisconsin. He is 53 yrs old. He can read and write and is now able to speak English; Mother tongue is listed as German; he arrived 1810?? And he is a farmer.

1930 US Census

1934 - 13 May. Lawrence died at the age of 58 (or 56) in the Town of Grant, Wisconsin.

Stevens Point Daily Journal 5/14/1934. Died yesterday (Sunday) at home in Grant. He had been in failing health for the past year...

Lawrence Disher, a resident of Portage county for many years, died Sunday night at 10 o'clock at his home in the town of Grant. He had been in failing health for the past year.

Mr. Disher was born on January 6, 1876, in Poland. He came to this country and located at Fancher. His marriage to Miss Mathilda Ostrowski took place at Plover on November 5, 1900. After their marriage the couple lived in Stevens Point. The family has lived in the town of Grant for the past 23 years.

Surviving are his wife, five daughters and five sons, Mrs. Charles Lubetski and Mrs. Joseph Wiater of Amherst Junction, Mrs. Bernard Shomberg of Custer, Mrs. Nicholas Washeliski of Hatley, John Disher of Stevens Point, and Jacob, Theodore, Bennie, Alois and Evelyn Disher at home. He is also survived by three sisters and three brothers, Mrs. Anton Kszonek of Amherst Junction, Mrs. John Singer and John Disher of

Wisconsin Rapids, Mrs. Michael Zbliski and F.S. Disher of Stevens Point and Jacob Disher of Fancher.

Funeral services will be held Wednesday morning at 10 o'clock at St. Bronislawa's church at Plover. Rev. W. B. Polaczyk will officiate and burial will take place in the parish cemetery. The body will be at the family home until the time of the funeral.

The Stevens Point Daily Journal of Thursday, May 17, 1934 adds:

...Rev. Frank S. Disher of Manitowoc, a nephew of the deceased, officiated at a requiem high mass... The pallbearers were Ted Disher, Jacob Disher, John Disher and Ben Disher, sons of the deceased, and Leo Singer and John Disher, nephews.

Relatives and friends from away who attended the funeral included Mr. and Mrs. Frank Disher, Mrs. Agnes Dudzek, Mrs. Mike Zbliski and Mr. and Mrs. John Kostuch of Stevens Point; Barney Shomberg of Milwaukee; Mr. and Mrs. Mike Walsheski of Hatley; Mr. and Mrs. Frank Ostrowski of Sharon; Mr. and Mrs. Joe Waeter, Mr. and Mrs. Charles Lubiecki and Mr. and Mrs. Jacob Disher...

Lawrence Disher

Lawrence Disher, a resident of Portage county for many years, died Sunday night at 10 o'clock at his home in the town of Grant. He had been in failing health for the past year.

Mr. Disher was born on January 6, 1876, in Poland. He came to this country and located at Fancher. His marriage to Miss Mathilda Ostrowski took place at Plover on November 5, 1900. After their marriage the couple lived in Stevens Point. The family has lived in the town of Grant for the past 23 years.

Surviving are his wife, five daughters and five sons, Mrs. Charles Lubetski and Mrs. Joseph Wiater of Amherst Junction, Mrs. Bernard Shomberg of Custer, Mrs. Nicholas Washeliski of Hatley, John Disher of Stevens Point and Jacob, Theodore, Bennie, Alois and Evelyn Disher at home. He is also survived by three sisters and three brothers, Mrs. Anton Kszonsk of Amherst Junction, Mrs. John Singer and John Disher of Wisconsin Rapids, Mrs. Michael Zbliski and F. S. Disher of Stevens Point and Jacob Disher of Fancher.

Funeral services will be held Wednesday morning at 10 o'clock at St. Bronislawa's church at Plover. Rev. W. B. Polaczyk will officiate and burial will take place in the parish cemetery. The body will be at the family home until the time of the funeral.

1934 - 16 May Burial St. Bronislawa's parish cemetery at Plover.

Lawrence's obituary and headstone shows date of birth as January 1876, which would make him 2 months older than his sister Clementine (her obituary says... "Mrs. Zblewski, the former Clementina Disher, was born in Poland on Nov. 23, 1875").

That is what makes genealogy so hard!

ANNA DISHER

ANNA M DISHER was born 13 Jun 1903 in Town of Plover, Portage County, WI., and died 26 Nov 1973 in West Plains, Howell County, MO.. She married (1) BERNARD C. SHOMBERG 07 Jan 1922 in St. Bronislava Catholic, Plover, Portage County, WI. He was born 03 Sep 1897 in Plainfield, Waushara County, WI., and died 03 Mar 1970 in Madison, Dade County, WI.. She married (2) Clark E. Vote. On 25 Jun 1972 in Ashtabula, OH. Mr. Vote died on 23 Sep 1981.

1973 - Obituary
Stevens Point Daily Journal
December 1, 1973 (Saturday)
Mrs. Clark Vote (nee Anna Disher)

Funeral services for Mrs. Clark Vote, 70, West Plains, MO and formerly of Plover, were held Thursday at the Schroeder Funeral Home, Madison.

Mrs. Vote died Monday (Nov 26) in West Plains, where another funeral service was held at the Carter Funeral Chapel Wednesday (Nov 28). Burial was in Memory Gardens, Madison.

The former Anna M. Disher was born June 13, 1903, in Plover, a daughter of Mr. and Mrs. Florian Disher, she married Bernard Schomberg (sic) on Jan. 7, 1922, in Plover. Her husband was a carpenter in the Stevens Point area until his death on March 3, 1970.

She was married June 13, 1972, to Clark E. Vote at Ashtabula, Ohio.

Survivors include her husband, her mother, Mrs. Mathilda Disher (Fredach), 418 5th Ave.; four sons, JOHN VICTOR, Bernard and Anthony Shomberg, Madison, and Joseph Shomberg, Miami, Fla.; three daughters, Mrs. Lorraine Buelow, Rothschild, Mrs. Irene Lang, Wisconsin Rapids, and Mrs. Theresa DeMerchant, Manus, Brazil; three brothers, Theodore Disher, 248 Franklin St., and Louis and John Disher , Milwaukee; three sisters, Mrs. Kathryn Waiter, 1732 Madison St., Mrs. Gertrude Schlickting, 418 5th Ave., and Mrs. Frances Washleski, Plover, 18 grandchildren and two great-grandchildren.

Preceded her in death were her father, her first husband, and one sister, two brothers and one son.

Mrs. Vote was a member of the Pentecostal Church.
Burial: 29 Nov 1973, Memory Gardens, Madison, Dane County, WI.

7. THE DOMBROWSKIS-KLOPOTEKS

JOHANN DOMBROWSKI. He married JULIANNA BOJAN PUCDROWSKI about 1795. Julianna was the daughter of CARL BOJAN (BOJANOVA) PUCDROWSKI (1768-1828) and CONSTANTIA KRECKA and she died August 18, 1845. Johann died 8 Sep 1852 in Borrek, Kreis Karthaus, Westpreußen (now Borek, Pomeranian Voivodeship, Poland)

Johann Dombrowski and Julianna Bojan Pucdrowski had the following children:

1.   Johann von Dombrowski b: ABT 1816

2.   Anton von Dombrowski b: 17 JAN 1817 in Borrek, Kreis Karthaus, Westpreußen (now Borek, Pomeranian Voivodeship, Poland). LDS Film 0072747: Catholic Church Records, Sullenschin, Westpreußen

3.   Joseph Theodore von Dombrowski b: 22 MAR 1821 in Borrek Szlachny, Kreis Karthaus, Westpreußen (now Borek, Pomeranian Voivodeship, Poland).

4.   Franz von Dombrowski b: 13 MAR 1823 in Borrek Nobilium, Kreis Karthaus, Westpreußen (now Borek, Pomeranian Voivodeship, Poland).

5.   AUGUSTIN VON DOMBROWSKI b: ABT 1824 in Rzeszów, Podkarpackie, Poland. He died on 05 Oct 1901 in Wisconsin, United States. He married ANTONINA VON KLOPOTEK, daughter of MICHAL KLOPOTEK (Dabrowski) and KATARZYNA BRONK ZDUNOWSKI in 1843. She was born in 1819 in Rzeszów, Podkarpackie, Poland. She died

on 05 Nov 1901 in Portage, Wisconsin

6.   Xavier von Dombrowski b: 22 JAN 1825 in Borrek Nobilium, Kreis Karthaus, Westpreußen (now Borek, Pomeranian Voivodeship, Poland).

7.   Thecla Rozalia von Dombrowski b: 30 AUG 1826 in Borrek, Kreis Karthaus, Westpreußen (now Borek, Pomeranian Voivodeship, Poland).

8.   Augustina Paulina von Dombrowski b: 29 MAR 1829 in Borrek, Kreis Karthaus, Westpreußen (now Borek, Pomeranian Voivodeship, Poland).

1845 – August 18 Death Of Julianna Bojan Pucdrowski per LDS Film 0072748: Catholic Church Records, Sullenschin, Westpreußen (now Suleczyno, Gdansk, Poland).
     "50 y/o at time of death on 8/18/1845". Children living at the time are listed as:
     1. Johann age 29
     2. Anton age 26
     3. August age 25
     4. Joseph age 23
     5. Franz age 21
     6. Thecla age 18
     7. Augustina age 16

1852 – September 8 – Death of Johann von Dombrowski per LDS Film 0072748: Catholic Church Records, Sullenschin, Westpreußen (now Suleczyno, Gdansk, Poland).   "70 y/o at time of death on 9/8/1852." Children living at the time are listed as:
     1. Johann age 36
     2. Anton age 33
     3. August age 32
     4. Joseph age 30
     5. Franz age 28
     6. Thecla age 25

AUGUSTIN   DOMBROWSKI was born in 1824 in Rzeszów, Podkarpackie, Poland. He died on 05 Oct 1901 in Wisconsin, United States. He married ANTONINA VON KLOPOTEK, daughter of MICHAL KLOPOTEK DABROWSKI (1782-1835) and KATARZYNA BRONK ZDUNOWSKI (1792-1853) in 1843. She was born in 1819 in Rzeszów, Podkarpackie, Poland. She died on 05 Nov 1901 in Portage, Wisconsin.

Marriage records: LDS Film 0072748: Catholic Church Records,

Sullenschin, Westpreußen (now Suleczyno, Gdansk, Poland).
Title: Pomeranian Marriage Indexes Author: PTG Pomorskie
Towarzystwo Genealogiczne
Publication: http://www.ptg.gda.pl
Suleczyno 1843 168 Augustinum Dabrowski-Antonina Klopotek

Augustin Dombrowski and Antonina Von Klopotek had the following
children:

1.   EMILIA (EMILIJA) ANTONINA DOMBROWSKI was born
on 14 Apr 1844 in Village of Borek, District of Karthaus, Province of
Gdansk, Poland (Godfather: Joseph Bronk of Bukowogora. Godmother:
Caterina Kreff of Szakau). She died on 09 May 1918 in Plover, Wisconsin,
Portage County.

2.   Theophil Mathias Dombrowski b: 8 FEB 1847 in Borrek, Kreis
Karthaus, Westpreußen (now Borek, Pomeranian Voivodeship, Poland).
Died 17 NOV 1848 in Borrek, Kreis Karthaus, Westpreußen (now Borek,
Pomeranian Voivodeship, Poland

3.   Joseph Franz Dombrowski b: 25 MAR 1849 in Borrek, Kreis
Karthaus, Westpreußen (now Borek, Pomeranian Voivodeship, Poland).

4.   August Dombrowski b: 27 AUG 1851 in Borrek, Kreis Karthaus,
Westpreußen (now Borek, Pomeranian Voivodeship, Poland). D. 22 Jan
1933

5.   Josephine Augustine Dombrowski b: 27 JUN 1854 in Borrek,
Kreis Karthaus, Westpreußen (now Borek, Pomeranian Voivodeship,
Poland).

6.   Anton Dombrowski b: 13 FEB 1857 in Borrek, Kreis Karthaus,
Westpreußen (now Borek, Pomeranian Voivodeship, Poland).

7.   Marcelli (Martin) Anton Dombrowski b: 17 FEB 1858 in Borrek,
Kreis Karthaus, Westpreußen (now Borek, Pomeranian Voivodeship,
Poland).

8.   Johann Ignacy Dombrowski b: 13 OCT 1860 in Borrek, Kreis
Karthaus, Westpreußen (now Borek, Pomeranian Voivodeship, Poland).

9.   Ignatius (Nick) Johann Dombrowski b: 3 MAY 1863 in Borrek,
Kreis Karthaus, Westpreußen (now Borek, Pomeranian Voivodeship,

Poland)..

ANTONINA VAN KLOPOTEK

1819 Birth of Antonina in Poland/Germany. Daughter of MICHAL KLOPOTEK DABROWSKI (1782-1835) and KATARZYNA BRONK ZDUNOWSKI (1792-1853).

1843 3 FEB marriage to Augustin Dombrowski in the Catholic Church at Sullenschin, Westpreußen (now Suleczyno, Pomeranian Voivodeship, Poland). Witnesses George Krefft and Anton Domaros

1901 5 OCT Antonina died in Stockton, Portage County, Wisconsin. (Title: Death Certificate - Antonia Dambrowski Note: Reel 109; Vol. 1; Pg 368; Image 0092; Seq. 074659 Repository:
Note: Wisconsin Historical Society)
Burial: 7 OCT 1901 Lake Thomas Cemetery, Stockton, Portage County, Wisconsin.

EMILIA (EMILIJA) ANTONINA DOMBROWSKI was born on 14 Apr 1844 in Village of Borek, District of Karthaus, Province of Gdansk, Poland (Godfather: Joseph Bronk of Bukowogora, Godmother: Caterina Kreff of Szakau). She died on 09 May 1918 in Plover, Wisconsin, Portage County. She married JACOB PHILIPP DISHER, son of FRANZ DISHER and MARIANNA ANNA WOSNIK on 08 Feb 1870 in Village of Suleczyno Catholic Church, District of Kaszuby, Gdansk Province, Poland. He was born on 30 Apr 1845 in Podjazy, District of Kartuzy, Gdansk Province, Poland (Naturalization papers says born abt 1844---1900 Census says born May 1846---January 1920 Census says age 74 last bday - 1845---family history says 1848---Disher online says 1846 .). He died on 05 Dec 1931 in Plover, Wisconsin, Portage County (Age: 75).

Emilia Dombroski Disher 1910

Emilia's obituary in the Gazette, Stevens Point, Wisconsin 1918 lists her surviving brothers as August of Plover, Martin of Hammond, Indiana. and Nick of Fancher.

DIES

Dies at
'ter

erchant
for 35
Church
morn-
s of 25
lthough
or only
d with
ith pa-

was 73
orn in
5. Af-
l of his
om the
college,
he was
e west,
here he
McKee
re. At
s Olive
r mar-
cert
ler was
for 11
s they
e Mr.
re and
home,
Pont,
spent
sh. Mr.
ears in
a part
Strongs
site of
garage.
ng the

in the
Fellows
ugh by.
had a

FATAL PARALYTIC STROKE

Mrs. Jacob Disher Succumbs Last Friday Morning After a Week's Illness

Mrs. Jacob Disher, a resident of Portage county for 37 years and for the past eighteen months living in Plover village, died at her home last Friday morning and was buried from the Fancher Catholic church at 10 o'clock on Monday, with interment in the parish cemetery. Just a week before she suffered a stroke of paralysis at work about her household work and remained in a semiconscious condition until the end. Her entire right side was affected. The lady had not been in good health for several months but she was up and around every day and felt fairly well until the fatal attack.

Mrs. Disher was a native of Poland, born there 74 years ago, and was married in her native land in 1870. The family came to America nine years later and settled on a homestead near Fancher station, town of Stockton, where the parents lived continuously until they retired from active pursuits last year.

Surviving children are Jos. Disher of Plover, Lawrence and John of Meehan, Jacob of Fancher, Frank S. of Nekoosa, Mrs. Anton Kazosh of New Hope, Mrs. John Singer of Meehan and Mrs. Mike Ziebowski of this city.

She also leaves three brothers, Martin Dombrowski of Hammond, Ind., August of Plover and Nick Dombrowski of Fancher.

The funeral services were largely attended and attested to the esteem in which this good lady was held by the friends she had known for so many years.

ROSSIER IN ENGLAND

Emil Rossier, son of Mr. and Mrs.

8. THE KIEDROWSKIS-OSTROWSKIS

MARTIN KIEDROWSKI was born in Poland. He died on 30 Apr 1857 in Tuschkau, Lippusch, Koscierzyna, Prussia. He married VICTORIA MASCHKE. She was born in Germany. NOTE: In Lipusz church records, the surname is also spelled Maszk and Maszke.

MARTIN KIEDROWSKI and VICTORIA MASCHKE had the following child:

ANDREW "ANORZEJ" KIEDROWSKI was born on October 29, 1821, in Germany, the only child of MARTIN and VICTORIA. He married JOSEPHINE CYBULSKA about 1851 and they had two sons and four daughters together. JOSEPHINE died after the birth of Julia in 1867 and before 1870 Census. He then married Magdalena Bemowski in 1870 in Stevens Point, Wisconsin. He died on December 30, 1895, in Bevent, Wisconsin, at the age of 74.

1851 Marriage to Josephine Cybulska

ANDREW "ANORZEJ" KIEDROWSKI and JOSEPHINE CYBULSKA had the following 6 children:

1. Mary Kiedrowski/Stroik was born in 1852 in Prussia. She died in 1887 in Wisconsin. And according to the 1880 Census, they had 5 children:

   Frank Stroick   b.1871
   John Stroick   b.1873
   Paul Stroick   b.1875
   Francis Stroick b.1877
   Mary Stroick   b.1879

2.   Paul Kiedrowski was born in 1853, in Prussia. He married Mary Kedrowski and they had 9 children:

> Veronica Kedrowski 1880 – ?
> Peter Kedrowski 1883 – ?
> John Kedrowski 1889 – ?
> Teclia Kedrowski 1892 – ?
> Matilda Kedrowski 1893 – ?
> Martha Kedrowski 1894 – ?
> Katie Kedrowski 1896 – ?
> Helena Kedrowski 1898 – ?
> August Kedrowski 1902 – ?

3.   Joseph Kiedrowski was born in 1856 in Prussia (was 4 yrs old in 1860 census). He married Mary Moskowski and they had 2 children:

> Anastasia "Stella" A. Kiedrowski 1915 – 1994
> Anton "Tony" Alois Kiedrowski 1918 – 2001

4.   FRANCES KIEDROWSKI was born in 1860 in Minnesota, United States. She died on 25 Feb 1952 in Sharon, Portage, Wisconsin, United States.

5.   Rosa Kiedrowski 1862-1906. She married Anton Anthony Sr Cyra Cera and they had 16 children:

> Joannes Cyra Cera 1880 – 1880
> Petrus Cyra Cera 1881 – 1881
> Franciscus Felix Cyra Cera 1883 – 1883
> Mary Cyra Cera 1885 – 1963
> David Paul Cyra Cera 1886 – 1935
> Agnes Cyra Cera 1887 – 1964
> John Cyra Cera 1889 – 1908
> Edward Cyra Cera 1891 – 1972
> Michael "Mike" Cyra Cera 1893 – 1979
> Joseph Cyra Cera 1896 – 1978
> Antony Cyra Cera 1898 – 1910
> Rosa Cyra Cera 1899 – ?
> Stanislaus "Stanley" B Cera 1900 – 1981
> Jacob "Jack" Cyra Cera 1902 – 1980
> Geo Cyra Cera 1902 – ?
> Magdeline (Margaret) Cyra Cera 1904 – 1974

6.   Julia Kiedrowski was born in 1867. No other records.

1859 Naturalization

Minnesota Naturalization Records Index, 1854-1957 about Andreas Kiedrowski

Name: Andreas Kiedrowski County: Winona Reel: 1 Code: 2 Volume: A Page: 9 Document Type: Declaration of Intention Years: 1858 -1872 Numbers: 1-592

First Papers, Winona, Winona County, Minnesota

1860 – July 6th, Andrew Radorka (sic) was 28 years old and lived in the 3rd Ward of the City of Winona, Minnesota. He was a day laborer. He lived with his wife Josephine (26 yrs old) and the children Mary (11 yrs old), Paul (7 yrs old), Joseph (4 yrs old) and Frances (4 months old)

6 Andrew Radorka	28	m		Day Laborer
Josephine "	26	F		
Mary "	11	"		
Paul "	7	m		
Joseph "	4	"		
Frances "	4/12	F		

1860 United States Federal Census

1870 – June 22nd, Andrew Kedrowsky (sic) was 45 years old and lived in Sharon, Wisconsin. He was a farmer. His real estate was valued at $1,800.00 and his personal estate valued at $750.00. He lived with Margeret (19 yrs old and keeping house) and older children Mary (17 yrs old – that does not match with previous Census, she should be 21 yrs old), Joseph (13 yrs old), Frances (10 yrs old), Roza (8 yrs old) and Julia (3 yrs old). All children, except Mary and Julia were at school. Paul is no longer living at home.

[census record image]

1870 United States Federal Census

1880 – June 7th, Andrew lives in Sharon with wife Maggie (age 34), Josephine's daughter Julia (13 yrs old) and 4 young children; Anna (9 yrs old), Catherine (7 yrs old), Joseph (4 yrs old) and Antonia (2 yrs old). His mother in law Catherine, also lives with him. He lists no employment.

[census record image]

1880 US Federal Census

1895 – June 20, Andrew Kiedrowski lived in Marathon, Wisconsin in a household counting 3 males and 3 females, 4 of which were born in the US.

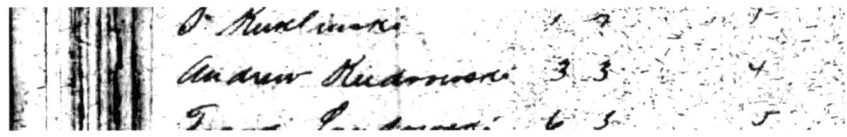

Wisconsin, State Censuses, 1895 and 1905

1895 – December 30th – Andrew is dead at age 74 in Tn Pike Lake (Bevent), Marathon County, Wisconsin

1896 January – Burial at St. Ladislaus Parish, Hatley, Wisconsin

His tombstone says:

URODZONI (born) WR (in) 1821
UMAR (died)
30 GRUDNIA (30 December)
ROKU (year) 1895

FRANCES KIEDROWSKI

When FRANCES KIEDROWSKI was born in 1860 in Minnesota, her father, ANDREW, was 38 and her mother, JOSEPHINE, was 26. She married LOUIS (LEON) OSTROWSKI on January 29, 1877, in Wisconsin. LOUIS was the son of NICK OSTROWSKI and CAROLINE RAKOWSKI. He was born in 1846 in Poland. They had seven children in 17 years.

Timeline for Frances Kiedrowski

1860 Born in the 3rd Ward, City of Winona, Minnesota, United States per 1860 Census where she is listed in her father's household [last name Radorka/Kiedrowski] as four months old in July. Her three older siblings and mother Josephine are listed as born in Germany. In the 1870 Census she is still listed as born in Minnesota and her older siblings in Prussia. That changed in the 1880 Census where she list Poland (?) as her place of birth.

1860 US Federal Census

1870 At the age of 10, Frances resided in Sharon, Portage, Wisconsin, United States with her family. The family moved to Wisconsin between 1867 and 1870.

1870 US Federal Census

1877 29 Jan Marriage to LOUIS (LEON) OSTROWSKI Age: 17 Wisconsin, USA

LOUIS (LEON) OSTROWSKI and FRANCES KIEDROWSKI had the following children:

1.	Theophilia Ostrowski was born on 08 Nov 1878 in Stockton, Portage, Wisconsin, United States. She died on 16 Jul 1936 in Appleton, Calumet, Wisconsin, United States and is buried at Saint Mary's Cemetery Torun Portage County Wisconsin, USA Plot: M. She married Max Waldoch and they had 9 children:
> Adam Waldoch 1897 – 1897
> Rose Waldoch 1898 – 1958
> Bernard L. Waldoch 1901 – 1966
> Barney Waldoch 1901 – ?
> Rudolph Waldoch 1903 – 1960
> Joseph Waldoch 1906 – 1984
> Peter Waldoch 1909 – 1973
> Helen Magdalen Waldoch 1912 – 1989
> Anastasia (Stella) Waldoch 1914 – 2007

2.	Felix Ostrowski was born on 20 Nov 1879 in Stockton, Portage, Wisconsin, United States. He died Feb 1964 in Milwaukee, Milwaukee, Wisconsin, United States. He spent 40 yrs (1934) as a patient in the Marshfield Hospital since taking a fall at the Biron Mill where he was a construction worker. He married Martha Hoffman and they had 4 children:
> Elizabeth Ostrowski 1898 –
> John Ostrowski 1907 –
> Sophia Ostrowski 1908 –
> Leo Ostrowski 1912 –

3.	MATHILDA OSTROWSKI/DISHER was born on 28 Feb 1882 in Ellis, Portage, Wisconsin, United States.

4.	Maryann Ostrowski was born on 10 Feb 1884 in Polonia, Wisconsin, United States. She died on 21 Sep 1966 in Iola, Waupaca, Wisconsin, United States. She married Frank M Ostrowski and they had 4 chldren:
> Herman Paul Ostrowski 1909 – 1960
> Helen Ostrowski/Kordus 1912 – ?
> Bernard Lawrence Ostrowski 1916 – 2001
> Amelia Ostrowski/Ramczyk 1918 – 1987

5.	Leon Leo Ostrowski/ was born on 25 Jan 1888 in Polonia, Portage, Wisconsin, United States. He died on 05 Dec 1930 in Milwaukee, Milwaukee, Wisconsin, United States. He married Regina Pelagia Helminiak

They had 3 children:
>> Frances Ostrowski 1914 – ?
>> Walter Ostrowski 1916 – ?
>> Raymond Ostrowski 1917 – ?

6. Martha Ostrowski was born in 1888 in Sharon, Portage, Wisconsin, United States. She died on 05 Sep 1910 in Stevens Point, Portage, Wisconsin, United States. She married Henry Kobak and they had 2 children:
>> Antone KOBAK 1907 – ?
>> Mary KOBAK 1908 – ?

7. Anastasia Ostrowski was born December 18, 1893 and died on July 20th, 1974 in Stevens Point, Portage, Wisconsin, USA. She married Frank W Ostrowski and they had 3 children:
>> Albert Ostrowski 1916 – ?
>> Alice Ostrowski 1918 – ?
>> Genevieve Ostrowski 1919 – ?

1880 – June 21st, Francis Ostriski (sic)was 24 years old and lived in Stockton, Wisconsin with her husband, Louis (age 34), daughter Feena (age 2) and son Felix (age 7 months). Louis was a farmer and she kept home. They both claim to be born in Poland and the children in Wisconsin.

Note that age does not match year of birth, should be 20 yrs old; also place of birth changed from Minnesota to Poland.

1880 US Federal Census

Before 1907 – Death - Frances and Leon died before 1907, per daughter Martha's and son-in-law Frank Ostrowski's obituaries. No other records (Census) can be found for them between 1880 and 1907. Some family trees give her date of death as 1903.

MATHILDA OSTROWSKI

MATHILDA OSTROWSKI was born on 28 Feb 1882 in Ellis, Portage, Wisconsin, United States. When her father Leon was 36 yrs old and her mother Frances was 22 yrs old.

1900 - She married (1) LAWRENCE (FLORIAN) DISHER, son of JACOB PHILIPP DISHER and EMILIA (EMILIJA) DOMBROWSKI on 05 Nov 1900 in St. Bronislva Catholic, Plover, Portage County, WI.

She married (2) JOSEPH FREDACH on 03 May 1937 in Plover, Portage, Wisconsin, United States. He was born on 25 Apr 1876 in Sharon, Portage, Wisconsin, United States. He died on 19 Feb 1954 in Marshfield, Wood, Wisconsin, United States

1993 - MATILDA OSTROWSKI DISHER FREDACH
Birth: Feb. 28, 1882 Death: Mar. 16, 1993
*Social Security Death Index
Name: Matilda Fredach
Last Residence: 54481 Stevens Point, Portage, Wisconsin, United States of America
Born: 28 Feb 1882
Died: 16 Mar 1993
State (Year) SSN issued: Wisconsin (1974)

OBITUARY

Wisconsin State Journal (Madison, WI) - March 17, 1993
ONE OF STATE'S OLDEST RESIDENTS DIES AT 111
Matilda "Tillie" Fredach, Portage County's oldest known resident, died Tuesday at age 111.

Fredach, a former homesteader and lifelong county resident, died at the Portage County Health Care Center where she had lived for 11 years.

"She was happy-go-lucky," said Charlene Cyran, a nurse who cared for her since she came to the center. "Everyone really loved her. She was the mascot of the wing."

Fredach was active and would rise each morning at 6, did not like to take naps and would go to bed at about 8 p.m., Cyran said.

"She never complained, and she liked to go, go go," she said. "She was a very active lady. She loved babies and animals."

Fredach, who celebrated her birthday last month with cake and coffee at an open house, was among a handful of Wisconsin residents who were 109 or older, state census figures showed.

Although she had some trouble with her hearing, eyesight and mobility, Fredach had a good appetite and was not often ill, workers at the center said.

Fredach was born Feb. 28, 1882, in Polonia and grew up speaking Polish. She attended rural schools.

She married on Nov. 5, 1900, to Florian Disher and the couple farmed in the town of Plover, where they homesteaded on 40 acres. He died in 1934.

In 1940, she married Joseph Fredach. He died in 1954.

Fredach raised 10 children and is survived by a son, a daughter, 63 grandchildren, 158 great-grandchildren, 73 great-great-grandchildren and six great-great-great grandchildren.

Her newest great-great grandchild, a girl, was born Tuesday.

Funeral services will be 10 a.m. Thursday at St. Bronislava Church in Plover. Burial will be in the parish cemetery.

Burial: Saint Bronislava Catholic Cemetery
Plover, Portage County, Wisconsin, USA

9. SOURCES

1820 United States Federal Census (Provo, UT, USA, Ancestry.com Operations, Inc., 2010)

1830 United States Federal Census (Provo, UT, USA, Ancestry.com Operations, Inc., 2010)

1840 United States Federal Census (Provo, UT, USA, Ancestry.com Operations, Inc., 2010)

1850 United States Federal Census (Provo, UT, USA, Ancestry.com Operations, Inc., 2009)

1860 United States Federal Census (Provo, UT, USA, Ancestry.com Operations, Inc., 2009)

1870 United States Federal Census (Provo, UT, USA, Ancestry.com Operations, Inc., 2009)

1900 United States Federal Census (Provo, UT, USA, Ancestry.com Operations Inc, 2004)

1910 United States Federal Census (Provo, UT, USA, Ancestry.com Operations Inc, 2006)

1920 United States Federal Census (Provo, UT, USA, Ancestry.com Operations Inc, 2010)

1930 United States Federal Census (Provo, UT, USA, Ancestry.com

Operations Inc, 2002)

1940 United States Federal Census (Provo, UT, USA, Ancestry.com Operations, Inc., 2012)

Ancestry Family Trees (Online publication - Provo, UT, USA: Ancestry.com. Original data: Family Tree files submitted by Ancestry members.). These information comes from 1 or more individual Ancestry Family Tree files. This source citation points you to a current version of those files. Note: The owners of these tree files may have removed or changed information since this source citation was created.

Appleton Post Crescent (Appleton, Wisconsin) (Online publication - Provo, UT, USA: Ancestry.com Operations Inc, 2006.Original data - Appleton Post Crescent. Appleton, WI, USA. Database created from microfilm copies of the newspaper. Original data: Appleton Post Crescent. Appleton, WI, USA. Database created)

Baltimore, Passenger Lists, 1820-1948 and 1954-1957 (Provo, UT, USA, Ancestry.com Operations Inc, 2006)

Florida Death Index, 1877-1998 (Online publication - Provo, UT, USA: Ancestry.com Operations Inc, 2004.Original data - State of Florida. Florida Death Index, 1877-1998. Florida: Florida Department of Health, Office of Vital Records, 1998.Original data: State of Florida. Florida Death Ind.

Central WI Genealogical Index

Gazette (Stevens Point, Wisconsin) (Online publication - Provo, UT, USA: The Generations Network, Inc., 2003.Original data - Gazette. Stevens Point, WI, USA. Database created from microfilm copies of the newspaper. Original data: Gazette. Stevens Point, WI, USA. Database created from microfilmed)

Genealogical Library Master Catalog (Online publication - Provo, UT, USA: The Generations Network, Inc., 1999.Original data - Crume, Rick. Genealogical Library Master Catalog. Original data: Crume, Rick. Genealogical Library Master Catalog. Vol. 1, November 1998 edition)

Gale Research, Passenger and Immigration Lists Index, 1500s-1900s (Online publication - Provo, UT, USA: Ancestry.com Operations, Inc, 2010.Original data - Filby, P. William, ed. Passenger and Immigration Lists Index, 1500s-1900s. Farmington Hills, MI, USA: Gale Research,

2010.Original data: Filby, P. William, ed. Passenge)

Godfrey Memorial Library, comp., American Genealogical-Biographical Index (AGBI) (Online publication - Provo, UT, USA: Ancestry.com Operations Inc, 1999.Original data - Godfrey Memorial Library. American Genealogical-Biographical Index. Middletown, CT, USA: Godfrey Memorial Library. Original data: Godfrey Memorial Library. American Genealogy)

Golla Relatives History at Portage County Public Library Compiled by Agnes Kawleski-Golla before 12 Nov 1994

Heritage Consulting, Millennium File (Online publication - Provo, UT, USA: Ancestry.com Operations Inc, 2003.Original data - Heritage Consulting. The Millennium File. Salt Lake City, UT, USA: Heritage Consulting. Original data: Heritage Consulting. The Millennium File. Salt Lake City, UT, USA)

http://library.uwsp.edu/depts/archives/Cemetery, Portage County Cemetery Locator. _UID: 4E43D1F3-0210-4E19-AC5A-2F2217B07D3C

http://www.disheronline.com/

Mecklenburg-Schwerin Volkszählung, 1819 (Online publication - Provo, UT, USA: Ancestry.com Operations Inc, 2007.Original data - Mecklenburg-Schwerin (Großherzogtum), Volkszählungsamt. Volkszählung 1819. Landeshauptarchiv Schwerin. 2.21-4/4 Bevölkerungs, Geburts, Konfirmations, Heirats und Ster)

Mecklenburg-Schwerin, Germany, Census, 1919 (Provo, UT, USA, Ancestry.com Operations, Inc., 2010)

Minnesota Death Index, 1908-2002 (Online publication - Provo, UT, USA: Ancestry.com Operations Inc, 2001.Original data - State of Minnesota. Minnesota Death Index, 1908-1002. Minneapolis, MN, USA: Minnesota Department of Health. Original data: State of Minnesota. Minnesota Death Index, 1908)

Minnesota Territorial and State Censuses, 1849-1905 (Online publication - Provo, UT, USA: Ancestry.com Operations Inc, 2007.Original data - Minnesota Historical Society. Minnesota State Population Census Schedules, 1865-1905. St. Paul, MN, USA: Minnesota Historical Society, 1977. Microfilm. Reels 1-47 and 10)

Minnesota, Births and Christenings Index, 1840-1980 (Online publication - Provo, UT, USA: Ancestry.com Operations, Inc., 2011.Original data - "Minnesota Births and Christenings, 1840–1980."
Index. Family Search, Salt Lake City, Utah, 2009, 2010. Index entries derived from digital copies of original and compiled)

Minnesota, Marriage Collection, 1958-2001 (Provo, UT, USA, Ancestry.com Operations Inc, 2007),

Missouri Marriage Records, 1805-2002 (Online publication - Provo, UT, USA: Ancestry.com Operations, Inc., 2007.Original data - Missouri Marriage Records. Jefferson City, MO, USA: Missouri State Archives. Microfilm. Original data: Missouri Marriage Records. Jefferson City, MO, USA: Missouri State)

Myron Felckowski, MyronFelckowskiTree. _UID: 5798336E-C3FD-4A0D-99D5-E3FC9EE71A0B

National Archives and Records Administration, U.S. World War II Army Enlistment Records, 1938-1946 (Online publication - Provo, UT, USA: Ancestry.com Operations Inc, 2005.Original data - Electronic Army Serial Number Merged File, 1938-1946 [Archival Database]; World War II Army Enlistment Records; Records of the National Archives and Records Administration)

New York Passenger Lists, 1820-1957 (Online publication - Provo, UT, USA: Ancestry.com Operations, Inc., 2010.Original data - Passenger Lists of Vessels Arriving at New York, New York, 1820-1897; (National Archives Microfilm Publication M237, 675 rolls); Records of the U.S. Customs Service, R)

Oconto County Polish National Cemetery

Ohio Marriage Index, 1970, 1972-2007 (Provo, UT, Ancestry.com Operations, Inc, 2010)

Portage County Historical Society of Wisconsin - Abridged from Malcolm Rosholt Online Archives

Post Crescent (Appleton, Wisconsin) (Online publication - Provo, UT, USA: The Generations Network, Inc., 2006.Original data - Post Crescent. Appleton, WI, USA. Database created from microfilm copies of the newspaper. Original data: Post Crescent. Appleton, WI, USA. Database created from microfilm)

Racine, Wisconsin Directories, 1890, 1892 (Provo, UT, USA, The Generations Network, Inc., 2000)

Staatsarchiv Hamburg, Hamburger Passagierlisten, 1850-1934 (Online publication - Provo, UT, USA: Ancestry.com Operations Inc, 2008.Original data - Staatsarchiv Hamburg, Bestand: 373-7 I, VIII (Auswanderungsamt I). Mikrofilmrollen K 1701 - K 2008, S 17363 - S 17383, 13116 - 13183.Original data: Staatsarchiv Hamburg)

Social Security Death Index (Online publication - Provo, UT, USA: Ancestry.com Operations Inc, 2011.Original data - Social Security Administration. Social Security Death Index, Master File. Social Security Administration. Original data: Social Security Administration. Social Security D)

Stevens Point Journal, The (Stevens Point, Wisconsin) (Online publication - Provo, UT, USA: The Generations Network, Inc., 2006.Original data - The Stevens Point Journal. Stevens Point, WI, USA. Database created from microfilm copies of the newspaper. Original data: The Stevens Point Journal. Stevens Point, WI)

The Church of Jesus Christ of Latter-day Saints, 1880 United States Federal Census (Online publication - Provo, UT, USA. 1880 U.S. Census Index provided by The Church of Jesus Christ of Latter-day Saints © Copyright 1999 Intellectual Reserve, Inc. All rights reserved.

U.S. and Canada, Passenger and Immigration Lists Index, 1500s-1900s (Provo, UT, USA, Ancestry.com Operations, Inc, 2010)

U.S. City Directories, 1821-1989 (Provo, UT, USA, Ancestry.com Operations, Inc., 2011)

U.S. Naturalization Record Indexes, 1791-1992 (Indexed in World Archives Project) (Online publication - Provo, UT, USA: Ancestry.com Operations, Inc., 2010. This collection was indexed by Ancestry World Archives Project contributors in partnership with the following organizations: Anchorage Genealogical Society, California State Genealogic)

U.S. Passport Applications, 1795-1925 (Online publication - Provo, UT, USA: Ancestry.com Operations, Inc., 2007. Original data - Passport

Applications, 1795-1905. NARA Microfilm Publication M1372, 694 rolls. General Records Department of State, Record Group 59. National Archives, Washington, D.C)

U.S. Phone and Address Directories, 1993-2002 (Online publication - Provo, UT, USA: Ancestry.com Operations Inc, 2005.Original data - 1993-2002 White Pages. Little Rock, AR, USA: Acxiom Corporation. Original data)

U.S. Public Records Index, Volume 1 (Online publication - Provo, UT, USA: Ancestry.com Operations, Inc., 2010.Original data - Voter Registration Lists, Public Record Filings, Historical Residential Records, and Other Household Database Listings. Original data: Voter Registration Lists, Public)

U.S. Public Records Index, Volume 2 (Online publication - Provo, UT, USA: Ancestry.com Operations, Inc., 2010.Original data - Voter Registration Lists, Public Record Filings, Historical Residential Records, and Other Household Database Listings. Original data: Voter Registration Lists, Public)

U.S., Indexed County Land Ownership Maps, 1860-1918 (Online publication - Provo, UT, USA: Ancestry.com Operations, Inc., 2010.Original data - Various publishers of County Land Ownership Atlases. Microfilmed by the Library of Congress, Washington, D.C. Original data: Various publishers of County Land Ownership)

U.S., World War I Draft Registration Cards, 1917-1918 (Provo, UT, USA, Ancestry.com Operations Inc, 2005)

United States Obituary Collection (Online publication - Provo, UT, USA: Ancestry.com Operations Inc, 2006. Original data)

Web: Wisconsin, Find A Grave Index, 1836-2012

Wisconsin Births, 1820-1907 (Online publication - Provo, UT, USA: Ancestry.com Operations Inc, 2000.Original data - Wisconsin Department of Health and Family Services. Wisconsin Vital Record Index, pre-1907. Madison, WI, USA: Wisconsin Department of Health and Family Services Vital Records)

Wisconsin Death Index, 1959-1997 (Online publication - Provo, UT, USA: Ancestry.com Operations Inc, 2007.Original data - Wisconsin Vital

Records Office. Wisconsin Death Index, 1959-67, 1969-97. Madison, Wisconsin, USA: Wisconsin Department of Health. Original data: Wisconsin Vital Records O)

Wisconsin Deaths, 1820-1907 (Online publication - Provo, UT, USA: Ancestry.com Operations Inc, 2000.Original data - Wisconsin Department of Health and Family Services. Wisconsin Vital Record Index, pre-1907. Madison, WI, USA: Wisconsin Department of Health and Family Services Vital Re)

Wisconsin Marriages, 1973-1997 (Online publication - Provo, UT, USA: Ancestry.com Operations Inc, 2005.Original data - Wisconsin Department of Health and Family Services. Wisconsin Marriages, 1973-1978; Wisconsin Marriages, 1979-1997. Wisconsin, USA: Wisconsin Department of Health and Family)

Wisconsin Rapids Daily Tribune (Wisconsin Rapids, Wisconsin) (Online publication - Provo, UT, USA: Ancestry.com Operations Inc, 2006.Original data - Wisconsin Rapids Daily Tribune. Wisconsin Rapids, WI, USA. Database created from microfilm copies of the newspaper. Original data: Wisconsin Rapids Daily Tribune. Wisconsin)

Wisconsin, Births and Christenings Index, 1826-1908 (Online publication - Provo, UT, USA: Ancestry.com Operations, Inc., 2011.Original data - "Wisconsin Births and Christenings, 1826–1926." Index. Family Search, Salt Lake City, Utah, 2009, 2010. Index entries derived from digital copies of original and compiled)

Wisconsin, Compiled Census and Census Substitutes Index, 1820-1890 (Provo, UT, USA, Ancestry.com Operations Inc, 1999)

Wisconsin State Censuses, 1895 and 1905 (Online publication - Provo, UT, USA: Ancestry.com Operations Inc, 2007.Original data - Wisconsin. Wisconsin State Census, 1895 Microfilm, 10 reels. Wisconsin Historical Society, Madison, Wisconsin. Wisconsin State Census, 1905. Microfilm, 44 reel)

Wisconsin Genealogical Society

Yates Publishing, U.S. and International Marriage Records, 1560-1900 (Online publication - Provo, UT, USA: Ancestry.com Operations Inc, 2004.Original data - This unique collection of records was extracted from a variety of sources including family group sheets and electronic databases).

<u>NOTES</u>